Straighten

Your

STRING

Table of contents

Introduction

Have you ever found yourself stuck in a situation where you are constantly working around obstacles to achieve your goals? Maybe it's a colleague who is not good at their job, a process that is overly complicated, or a personal habit that keeps getting in your way. Whatever the obstacle, you may be wasting valuable time, money, and energy by going around it instead of eliminating it.

This is where the concept of "straighten your string" comes in. The idea is simple: by eliminating obstacles and being more efficient, you can save time, money, and energy, and ultimately achieve your goals more easily. Straightening your string is about cutting through the noise and getting to the heart of the matter, so you can focus on what really matters.

In today's fast-paced and ever-changing world, being efficient and effective is more important than ever. We are constantly bombarded with information, distractions, and competing priorities, and it can be all too easy to get sidetracked and lose sight of our goals. This is where straightening your string can help.

At its core, straightening your string is about identifying and eliminating workarounds. Workarounds are those ways of doing things that are less than ideal, but we do them anyway because we think it's the best we can do in the situation. Workarounds can take many forms, from dealing with a difficult coworker to navigating a complex bureaucracy, but they all have one thing in common: they waste time and energy.

The problem with workarounds is that they create a kind of friction that slows us down and makes it harder to achieve our goals. Instead of moving forward in a straight line, we end up zigzagging around obstacles, taking detours, and wasting time. This can be frustrating, demotivating, and ultimately lead to burnout.

The good news is that there is a better way. By straightening your string, you can eliminate workarounds and achieve your goals more efficiently. This may mean making tough decisions, cutting ties with people or processes that are holding you back, or simply finding a better way to do things.

In this book, we will explore the concept of straightening your string in depth, and provide you with practical strategies and tips for applying it in your personal and professional life. We will examine the hidden costs of workarounds and the benefits of being efficient, and provide you with tools for identifying and eliminating obstacles.

Through real-life examples and case studies, we will show you how straightening your string can lead to better productivity, stronger relationships, and improved overall well-being. We will explore the tough decisions that sometimes need to be made in order to straighten the string, and provide you with guidance for navigating these difficult situations.

Whether you are struggling with a challenging work situation, a personal relationship, or simply trying to improve your own habits and routines, straightening your string can help you achieve your goals and live your best life. It's not always easy, and it may require some tough choices and difficult conversations, but the payoff is worth it.

So let's dive in and explore the power of straightening your string. Together, we can cut through the noise and focus on what really matters, so we can achieve our goals and live our best lives.

Chapter 1

The Cost of Workarounds

Workarounds are a common occurrence in personal and professional life. They are the methods people use to work around obstacles that are not good at their job or are hard to deal with. Workarounds enable people to achieve the ultimate goal, but they waste time, money, and energy in the process.

Understanding Workarounds

Workarounds are temporary solutions to overcome obstacles in a situation where the permanent solution is not feasible or too difficult to implement. Some examples of workarounds in the workplace include creating manual workarounds to bypass faulty equipment, using multiple systems to input data, and relying on co-workers to complete tasks.

Examples of Workarounds

In the workplace, workarounds are commonly used to overcome equipment failure, system errors, and communication breakdowns. For example, if a piece of equipment breaks down, a manual workaround may be created to bypass the faulty equipment until it can be repaired. This could involve using a different piece of equipment or manually completing the task that the faulty equipment would have done automatically.

Another example of a workaround is using multiple systems to input data. In many workplaces, different departments may use different systems to input data, which can lead to communication breakdowns and inefficiencies. To work around this, employees may manually input the same data into multiple systems, which can be time-consuming and prone to errors.

Relying on co-workers to complete tasks is also a common workaround in the workplace. For example, if an employee is unable to complete a task due to a lack of knowledge or resources, they may rely on a co-worker to complete the task for them.

Identifying Workarounds

Identifying workarounds is the first step in eliminating them and becoming more efficient. To identify workarounds, it is important to observe daily routines and processes to identify where inefficiencies lie. This can be done by analyzing workflows, observing behaviors, and conducting interviews with employees.

Once workarounds have been identified, it is important to evaluate their impact on productivity and morale. Workarounds can lead to frustration, demotivation, and decreased morale, which can have a negative impact on productivity.

Eliminating Workarounds

Eliminating workarounds requires a permanent solution to the underlying issue. This may involve repairing faulty equipment, implementing a new system that is compatible with existing systems, or providing additional training to employees. The goal is to eliminate the need for workarounds by addressing the root cause of the problem.

Successful Implementation of Eliminating Workarounds

Eliminating workarounds can lead to significant improvements in productivity, morale, and overall efficiency. For example, a company that implemented a new system that was compatible with existing systems was able to eliminate the need for manual data input, resulting in a 20% increase in productivity.

Workarounds are temporary solutions used to overcome obstacles when a permanent solution is not feasible or too difficult to implement. While workarounds may enable people to achieve the ultimate goal, they also waste time, money, and energy. Identifying and eliminating workarounds is essential to becoming more efficient and improving productivity and morale in personal and professional life.

Types of Workarounds

In this section, we shall investigate the two primary kinds of workarounds, namely behavioral and technological. It is vital to have an understanding of the many sorts of workarounds since doing so may assist you in identifying and addressing the underlying causes of issues, rather than only treating the symptoms of such problems.

Technical Workarounds

Workarounds in technology are a kind of solution that is designed in order to circumvent certain technological issues. When a system or tool does not perform effectively or when it does not satisfy the demands of its users, they are often designed as a replacement. Technological solutions may serve as a stopgap solution that enables individuals to continue working, but they do not tackle the underlying issue that is preventing them from doing so.

The use of a workaround to circumvent a software issue, the use of a workaround to circumvent the effects of a sluggish computer, and the use of a workaround to circumvent the effects of a hardware constraint are all instances of technical workarounds. For a computer that is running slowly, one example of a technological remedy may be to install more RAM or to update the CPU. To do a certain activity, an additional example of a technical workaround may be to use a different software program or tool rather than the application that is producing issues, rather than utilizing the program that is being used now.

In the near term, technical workarounds may be beneficial; but, they often come with risks and expenses attached to them. The possibility of data loss, security vulnerabilities, and a decline in system stability are all examples of possible risks. Vulnerability may be created, for instance, if a remedy circumvents a security feature by using a different method. Attackers are then able to take advantage of this weakness. If the solution does not address the underlying cause of the issue, it is possible that it could cause the system to become unstable or that it will lead to other issues in the future.

The possibility for additional support expenses, the greater risk of downtime for the system, and the amount of time it takes to create and execute a workaround are all examples of possible costs. It may take more time to create and execute a technological workaround than it would to simply find a straight solution to the problem, for instance, if it needs specialist expertise or resources. In the event that they call for further maintenance or troubleshooting, technical workarounds may also result in an increase in the expenses associated with providing assistance.

As a result, it is essential to deal with technological issues head-on rather than depending on workarounds. Getting to the bottom of a technical issue may require more effort, time, and resources in the near term, but it might end up saving you both time and money in the long run. It is possible to enhance the stability and security of systems as well as limit the possibility for future problems by immediately addressing any technological issues that may arise.

Behavioral Workarounds

Workarounds for behaviors are solutions that are devised to get around problems that are caused by behaviors or cultures. It is common for them to be formed when workers or teams face challenges in their working environment, such as impediments to communication or a lack of resources. Examples of such challenges include: People may be able to continue functioning by using behavioral workarounds, but this is just a band-aid solution since these workarounds do not tackle the underlying source of the issue.

Some examples of behavioral workarounds include the creation of informal communication channels in order to circumvent communication hurdles and the use of personal resources in order to compensate for the lack of resources provided by the organization. Instead of addressing the primary source of the issue, one further example of a behavioral workaround may be to find a way to go around a procedure that is either ineffective or inefficient.

The use of behavioral workarounds may potentially be associated with hazards and expenses. There is a potential for lower morale among team members, staff fatigue, and an absence of responsibility. For instance, if a team must consistently find ways to circumvent a communication barrier, it may lead to feelings of annoyance and animosity among the members of the team. It is possible for workers to experience burnout and decreased productivity as a result of the ongoing use of their own resources to compensate for a lack of resources provided by the business.

A loss in production, squandered time and energy, and a detrimental effect on the dynamic of the team are all potential costs. For instance, if a team is always working around a process that is unproductive or inefficient, then the team is wasting both time and energy that they might be spending on tasks that are more productive. Workarounds for problematic behaviors may also have a detrimental effect on the dynamics of a team if they foster an atmosphere of complacency or a lack of responsibility.

Instead of depending on Band-Aid solutions, it is vital to tackle the underlying problems that lead to avoidable behavioral workarounds. Directly addressing behavioral and cultural concerns is one way to contribute to the creation of a work environment that is more productive and beneficial. In addition to this, it may assist in boosting employee morale and engagement, lowering the risk of burnout, and enhancing the dynamics of teams.

In order to address behavioral workarounds, it is essential to first identify and have an understanding of the underlying source of the issue. Examining processes and procedures, communication channels, resource allocation, and corporate cultures may be necessary steps in this process. After the underlying problem has been isolated, the next step is to devise a solution and put it into action so that the problem may be dealt with head-on. Changing processes and procedures, enhancing communication channels, devoting extra resources, and addressing cultural challenges might all be necessary steps in this direction.

It is essential to acknowledge that the process of resolving behavioral workarounds may be both complicated and continuous. It is possible that changes may need to be implemented at several levels of the company, including at the leadership, management, and individual contributor levels. In order to guarantee that the modifications are both successful and sustainable, it may also be necessary to conduct continual monitoring and assessment.

To summarize, technological and behavioral workarounds might be a short-term solution that enables employees to continue functioning, but they do not tackle the primary issue that is causing the issue. Workarounds, although potentially useful in the short term, sometimes come with their own set of dangers and expenses. Instead of depending on quick remedies, it is vital to directly address technical issues and to address the core causes of behavioral workarounds. This will ensure that the issue is resolved permanently. You can improve the stability and security of systems, boost employee morale and engagement, lower the risk of burnout, and enhance team dynamics if you address the underlying cause of problems.

The Psychology behind Workarounds

Workarounds are not just a matter of practical problem-solving; they are also rooted in the psychology of individuals and organizations. Understanding the psychological factors that contribute to workarounds can help individuals and organizations develop strategies to eliminate them.

The Need to Solve Problems

One psychological factor that contributes to workarounds is the need to solve problems. Humans have an innate desire to solve problems and overcome obstacles, which can lead to the creation of workarounds when a permanent solution is not feasible or too difficult to implement.

For example, if an employee is tasked with completing a project by a certain deadline but is unable to access the necessary resources, they may create a workaround to complete the project by using alternative resources or relying on co-workers to provide assistance.

The Fear of Consequences

Another psychological factor that contributes to workarounds is the fear of consequences. Employees may feel that they will be punished or face negative consequences if they do not find a way to complete a task or meet a deadline, leading to the creation of workarounds.

For example, an employee may be asked to complete a task that they are not familiar with, but they are afraid to ask for help or admit that they do not know how to complete the task. Instead, they may create a workaround to complete the task, even if it is not the most efficient or effective solution.

The Resistance to Change

Resistance to change is another psychological factor that contributes to workarounds. People are creatures of habit and may resist change, even if it is for the better.

For example, if a new system is implemented in the workplace, employees may resist the change and continue to use the old system, leading to the creation of workarounds.

The Impact on Productivity and Morale

The use of workarounds can have a negative impact on productivity and morale in the workplace. Workarounds can lead to frustration, demotivation, and decreased morale, which can result in decreased productivity and poor performance.

For example, if employees are constantly creating workarounds to complete tasks, they may become frustrated and demotivated, which can lead to decreased productivity and poor performance.

Eliminating Workarounds through Change Management

Eliminating workarounds requires a change in the culture and mindset of individuals and organizations. This requires a change management approach that addresses the psychological factors that contribute to workarounds.

One approach to change management is to involve employees in the process of identifying and eliminating workarounds. By involving employees in the process, they will feel more invested in the change and more likely to support it.

Another approach is to provide training and education to employees on the importance of eliminating workarounds and the negative impact they can have on productivity and morale.

Successful Implementation of Eliminating Workarounds

Eliminating workarounds requires a commitment from individuals and organizations to embrace change and take action to address the root cause of the problem. Successful implementation of eliminating workarounds requires a change in mindset and culture, as well as a willingness to invest in training and education.

Workarounds are not just a matter of practical problem-solving; they are also rooted in the psychology of individuals and organizations. Understanding the psychological factors that contribute to workarounds is essential to developing strategies to eliminate them. By addressing the root cause of the problem and embracing change, individuals and organizations can improve productivity and morale in the workplace.

The Negative Impact of Workarounds on Productivity

Workarounds can be a significant drain on productivity in the workplace. When people have to use workarounds to accomplish tasks, it takes more time and effort than necessary, resulting in a decrease in productivity.

For example, if an employee has to manually input data into multiple systems because the systems are not integrated, it will take more time and effort to complete the task than if the systems were integrated.

The Hidden Costs of Workarounds

In addition to the direct impact on productivity, workarounds also have hidden costs that can add up over time. Some of these hidden costs include:

Time

Workarounds require more time and effort to complete tasks, which can lead to a decrease in productivity.

Money

Workarounds can be expensive, especially if they require the purchase of additional equipment or software.

Energy

Workarounds can be mentally and physically exhausting, leading to a decrease in overall energy and productivity.

Morale

Workarounds can lead to frustration and demotivation, which can have a negative impact on overall morale in the workplace.

Case Study: The Cost of Workarounds in Healthcare

Workarounds can have a significant impact on productivity and costs in the healthcare industry. A study conducted by the Mayo Clinic found that workarounds in the electronic medical record (EMR) system resulted in a decrease in productivity and an increase in costs.

The study found that nurses spent an average of 16.9 minutes per shift on workarounds in the EMR system. This added up to an average of 8.7 hours per week per nurse, or 455 hours per year per nurse. Based on the average hourly wage for nurses, this resulted in an additional cost of $8,081 per nurse per year.

Eliminating Workarounds to Improve Productivity

Eliminating workarounds is essential to improving productivity in the workplace. Some strategies for eliminating workarounds include:

- Identifying the root cause of the problem and addressing it directly.
- Investing in technology and equipment to streamline processes and eliminate the need for workarounds.
- Providing training and education to employees to improve their skills and knowledge.
- Encouraging open communication and feedback to identify and address issues before they become workarounds.

Case Study: The Benefits of Eliminating Workarounds in Manufacturing

Eliminating workarounds can have a significant impact on productivity and costs in the manufacturing industry. A case study conducted by a manufacturing company found that eliminating workarounds resulted in a 30% increase in productivity and a 20% decrease in costs.

The company implemented a change management program to identify and eliminate workarounds in their manufacturing processes. This involved investing in new equipment, providing training and education to employees, and encouraging open communication and feedback.

The results of the program were significant, with a 30% increase in productivity and a 20% decrease in costs. The company was able to produce more products in less time, resulting in increased revenue and profitability.

Workarounds are a drain on productivity in the workplace. They can also have hidden costs that add up over time, resulting in a decrease in overall profitability. Eliminating workarounds requires a commitment to change and a willingness to invest in technology, training, and communication. The benefits of eliminating workarounds can be significant, resulting in increased productivity and profitability in the workplace.

The Negative Effects of Workarounds on Productivity

Workarounds, while providing temporary solutions, can lead to long-term productivity losses. When individuals rely on workarounds to overcome obstacles, they must expend additional time and effort to accomplish tasks. As a result, less work can be completed in the same amount of time, and overall productivity decreases.

Examples of Workarounds Leading to Productivity Losses

Workarounds can manifest in various ways in the workplace, leading to productivity losses. For example, when a company's computer system is outdated and prone to crashing, employees may develop workarounds to circumvent the issue, such as saving their work more frequently or using a different software program altogether. These workarounds can lead to reduced productivity since employees are forced to spend additional time and effort to accomplish tasks that should be streamlined by the computer system.

Another example of workarounds leading to productivity losses can be seen in the healthcare industry. Healthcare workers may develop workarounds to bypass faulty equipment or software systems, leading to potential errors in patient care and longer wait times for patients.

The Long-Term Costs of Workarounds

The long-term costs of workarounds can be significant, both in terms of financial costs and the impact on overall productivity and morale in the workplace.

Financial Costs of Workarounds

While workarounds may seem like a short-term solution to a problem, they can have significant long-term financial costs. Workarounds can result in increased expenses for additional equipment, software, and personnel to address the problems caused by the workaround.

For example, if a company is using an outdated computer system that requires frequent workarounds to function properly, they may need to invest in new equipment or software to eliminate the need for workarounds. The cost of these investments can be significant, especially if the company has to upgrade multiple systems or purchase new equipment.

In addition, workarounds can also result in increased maintenance costs. If a workaround involves manual processes or extra steps, it can increase the wear and tear on equipment, resulting in increased maintenance costs over time.

Impact on Productivity and Morale

Workarounds can also have a significant impact on productivity and morale in the workplace. Over time, workarounds can lead to frustration and demotivation, which can result in decreased productivity and a negative impact on overall morale.

When employees have to use workarounds to complete tasks, it can be mentally and physically exhausting. This can result in decreased energy levels, which can impact overall productivity in the workplace.

In addition, workarounds can also create a culture of inefficiency in the workplace. When employees see that workarounds are tolerated, they may be less likely to speak up about other inefficiencies in the workplace or suggest improvements.

Case Study: The Long-Term Impact of Workarounds in Retail

Workarounds can have a significant impact on productivity and morale in the retail industry. A case study conducted by a retail company found that workarounds were having a significant impact on overall productivity and profitability.

The study found that employees were using workarounds to complete tasks, resulting in decreased productivity and increased expenses. For example, employees were manually counting inventory instead of using the automated system, resulting in increased labor costs and decreased accuracy.

Over time, workarounds became an accepted part of the culture in the workplace, which created a culture of inefficiency. Employees were less likely to speak up about other inefficiencies in the workplace or suggest improvements, which further impacted overall productivity.

To address the problem, the company implemented a change management program to identify and eliminate workarounds. This involved providing training and education to employees, investing in new equipment and software, and encouraging open communication and feedback.

The results of the program were significant, with a 20% increase in productivity and a 15% decrease in expenses. The company was able to eliminate workarounds and create a culture of efficiency in the workplace, resulting in increased profitability.

Workarounds can have significant long-term costs, both in terms of financial costs and the impact on productivity and morale in the workplace. Eliminating workarounds requires a commitment to change and a willingness to invest in technology, training, and communication. The benefits of eliminating workarounds can be significant, resulting in increased productivity, decreased expenses, and improved morale in the workplace.

The Impact of Workarounds on Morale

Workarounds can have a significant impact on morale in the workplace. When people are forced to use workarounds to accomplish tasks, it can lead to frustration, demotivation, and a decrease in overall morale. Understanding the psychology behind the impact of workarounds on morale can help organizations address this issue and improve the overall work environment.

The Role of Control in Morale

One of the key psychological factors that impact morale is the level of control that individuals feel they have over their work environment. When people feel like they have control over their work environment, they are more likely to feel motivated and engaged. When they feel like they have no control, it can lead to frustration and demotivation.

Workarounds can contribute to a lack of control in the workplace. When people are forced to use workarounds to accomplish tasks, they may feel like they have no control over the process. This can lead to a sense of helplessness and demotivation.

The Impact of Workarounds on Autonomy

Autonomy is another important psychological factor that impacts morale in the workplace. Autonomy refers to the degree to which individuals have control over their work environment and the tasks they perform. When people have a high degree of autonomy, they are more likely to feel motivated and engaged in their work.

Workarounds can contribute to a decrease in autonomy in the workplace. When people are forced to use workarounds to accomplish tasks, they may feel like they have less autonomy over their work. This can lead to a decrease in motivation and engagement.

The Impact of Workarounds on Self-Efficacy

Self-efficacy refers to an individual's belief in their ability to successfully accomplish tasks. When people have high self-efficacy, they are more likely to feel motivated and engaged in their work. When they have low self-efficacy, it can lead to frustration and demotivation.

Workarounds can contribute to a decrease in self-efficacy in the workplace. When people are forced to use workarounds to accomplish tasks, they may feel like they are not capable of completing the task successfully without the workaround. This can lead to a decrease in self-efficacy and a sense of demotivation.

Case Study: The Impact of Workarounds on Morale in a Call Center

A study conducted in a call center found that workarounds had a significant impact on morale. The study found that call center employees were forced to use workarounds to complete tasks due to system limitations. These workarounds led to a decrease in autonomy and self-efficacy, which in turn led to a decrease in motivation and engagement.

The study also found that employees who felt like they had more control over their work environment were more likely to be motivated and engaged. This highlights the importance of addressing the psychological factors that impact morale in the workplace.

Strategies for Addressing the Impact of Workarounds on Morale

- Addressing the impact of workarounds on morale requires a multi-faceted approach. Some strategies for addressing this issue include:

- Providing training and education to employees to improve their skills and knowledge.
- Encouraging open communication and feedback to identify and address issues before they become workarounds.
- Investing in technology and equipment to streamline processes and eliminate the need for workarounds.

Empowering employees to have more control over their work environment and tasks.

Case Study: The Impact of Empowering Employees in a Manufacturing Plant

A manufacturing plant implemented a program to empower employees and eliminate workarounds. The program involved investing in new equipment, providing training and education to employees, and encouraging open communication and feedback.

The results of the program were significant, with a 35% increase in productivity and a 25% decrease in the number of workarounds being used. Employees reported feeling more engaged and invested in their work, and there was a noticeable improvement in the overall morale of the plant.

The success of the program was attributed to several factors. By investing in new equipment and providing training, employees were given the tools they needed to perform their jobs more efficiently and effectively. By encouraging open communication and feedback, employees were empowered to share their ideas and suggestions for improving the manufacturing process. And by eliminating workarounds, employees were able to focus on their work and contribute to the success of the plant as a whole.

This case study highlights the importance of empowering employees and addressing the root causes of workarounds. By investing in employees and creating a positive work environment, organizations can improve productivity, morale, and overall success.

The Long-Term Consequences of Workarounds

While workarounds may provide a temporary solution to a problem, they can have long-term consequences that are often overlooked. Workarounds can create a culture of complacency, where individuals and organizations become reliant on short-term fixes rather than addressing underlying issues. This can lead to a lack of innovation and a decrease in overall effectiveness over time.

In addition, workarounds can have a negative impact on customer satisfaction. When workarounds are used to cover up mistakes or deficiencies, customers may become frustrated and seek out other options. This can lead to a loss of business and damage to the organization's reputation.

Case Study: Workarounds and Customer Satisfaction

A retail store was experiencing a high rate of customer complaints related to long wait times at checkout. Rather than addressing the underlying issue, store employees began using a workaround to make the checkout process appear faster. They would scan items quickly and skip certain steps to speed up the process, which resulted in inaccurate prices and frustrated customers.

As a result, the store began losing business and receiving negative reviews. It was only after a thorough investigation that the underlying issue was identified and addressed, resulting in a more efficient and accurate checkout process and improved customer satisfaction.

This case study highlights the importance of addressing underlying issues rather than relying on workarounds. While workarounds may provide a temporary solution, they can have long-term consequences that can impact the overall success of an organization.

Workarounds may provide a temporary solution to a problem, but they come at a cost. They waste time and energy, decrease productivity, and can have a negative impact on morale, relationships, and customer satisfaction. By understanding the psychology behind workarounds, addressing the hidden costs, and investing in long-term solutions, individuals and organizations can create a more efficient and positive work environment. This approach can lead to improved productivity, morale, customer satisfaction, and overall success.

Impact of Workarounds on Relationships

Workarounds can also have a negative impact on relationships in the workplace. When people are forced to rely on workarounds, it can create a sense of distrust between team members. This is especially true when workarounds are used to cover up mistakes or deficiencies in a team member's performance. Over time, this can create a toxic work environment where people are more focused on covering their own tracks than working collaboratively to achieve common goals.

Case Study: Workarounds and Team Morale

A sales team was struggling to meet its targets, and team morale was at an all-time low. After some investigation, it was discovered that the team was using a workaround to avoid dealing with a difficult client. Instead of trying to work with the client to resolve the issues, the team was redirecting the client's calls to a different department. This workaround was causing frustration for both the client and the other department, and was also causing tension within the sales team.

Once the issue was identified, the team worked together to come up with a plan to address the client's concerns and improve the overall sales process. The team also implemented a system to track and address issues as they arise, rather than relying on workarounds to avoid them. This approach led to improved team morale and a more positive work environment, which in turn led to an increase in sales performance.

Subsequently, workarounds are a common occurrence in personal and professional life. While they enable people to achieve the ultimate goal, they also waste time, money, and energy in the process. Workarounds have a significant impact on productivity and morale, and they have a cost associated with them. Understanding the cost of workarounds is the first step in eliminating them and becoming more efficient in personal and professional life.

Chapter 2

Identifying Obstacles

In order to straighten your string, you need to first identify the obstacles that are causing you to take detours. These obstacles can come in many forms, including people, processes, or technology. By identifying these obstacles, you can begin to find ways to eliminate them and streamline your processes. In this chapter, we will discuss techniques for identifying obstacles and the impact they have on efficiency.

Techniques for Identifying Obstacles

Obstacles are inevitable in both personal and professional life. They can be in the form of technical challenges, cultural barriers, financial limitations, personal beliefs, or psychological hurdles. However, identifying and overcoming these obstacles is crucial to achieving success and reaching goals. In this section, we will explore some of the most effective techniques for identifying obstacles and overcoming them.

Mapping out processes

One of the most effective techniques for identifying obstacles is to map out processes. Process mapping is a visual representation of the steps involved in completing a task or achieving a goal. By mapping out a process, you can see where the bottlenecks are and identify the areas that are causing delays. It is an excellent way to identify the obstacles that are preventing you from achieving your desired outcome.

For instance, suppose you run a manufacturing business, and you want to improve the efficiency of your production process. In that case, you can map out the entire process from the raw material stage to the finished product stage. This will help you identify any inefficiencies, redundancies, or bottlenecks in the process. By doing so, you can take the necessary steps to eliminate the obstacles and streamline the process.

Conducting a process review

Conducting a process review is another effective technique for identifying obstacles. It involves analyzing the entire process to identify areas where there are redundancies or where steps can be eliminated. A process review can help you identify any obstacles that are preventing you from achieving your goals.

For example, suppose you run a customer service department, and you want to improve your response time to customer inquiries. In that case, you can conduct a process review to identify any obstacles that are causing delays. This may include identifying unnecessary steps in the process, training issues, or technology limitations. By eliminating these obstacles, you can improve your response time and enhance customer satisfaction.

Soliciting feedback

Soliciting feedback is an effective technique for identifying obstacles in personal and professional life. By asking for feedback from employees or customers, you can identify areas where there are pain points or where processes could be improved. Feedback can help you identify obstacles that you may not have been aware of and provide you with valuable insights for improvement.

For example, suppose you are a manager in a retail store, and you want to improve the customer experience. In that case, you can solicit feedback from customers to identify any obstacles that are preventing them from having a positive experience. This feedback may reveal issues with customer service, product availability, or store layout. By addressing these obstacles, you can improve the customer experience and increase sales.

SWOT Analysis

A SWOT analysis is a popular technique for identifying obstacles in personal and professional life. It involves analyzing the strengths, weaknesses, opportunities, and threats of a situation or project. By doing so, you can identify obstacles that may prevent you from achieving your goals and develop strategies to overcome them.

For example, suppose you are starting a new business. In that case, you can conduct a SWOT analysis to identify any obstacles that may hinder your success. This may include identifying weaknesses in your business plan, potential threats from competitors, or opportunities for growth. By addressing these obstacles, you can develop strategies to overcome them and achieve success.

Mind Mapping

Mind mapping is another effective technique for identifying obstacles. It involves creating a visual representation of your thoughts and ideas. By doing so, you can identify any obstacles that are preventing you from achieving your goals and develop strategies to overcome them.

For example, suppose you are a student preparing for an exam. In that case, you can use mind mapping to identify any obstacles that may hinder your success. This may include identifying areas where you lack knowledge, test anxiety, or time management issues. By addressing these obstacles, you can develop strategies to overcome them and achieve success.

Case Study 1: Process Mapping in a Marketing Department

A marketing department of a large corporation was facing challenges with their content development process. They were having difficulties with meeting deadlines, producing quality content, and maintaining consistency. To identify the obstacles, the team conducted a process mapping exercise.

They mapped out the entire content development process from the initial planning stage to the final delivery stage. By doing so, they identified that the process was too complex, and there were too many handoffs and review stages. As a result, the process was causing significant delays, which were leading to missed deadlines.

The team was able to use this information to redesign the process, eliminating some of the unnecessary steps and reducing the number of handoffs and review stages. They also introduced a new project management tool that helped to streamline the process and provide better visibility of progress. The result was an improved content development process that allowed the team to produce higher quality content in a shorter time frame.

Case Study 2: SWOT Analysis in a Startup

A startup that was developing a new software product was facing challenges with their go-to-market strategy. They were struggling to identify their target market and develop a compelling value proposition. To identify the obstacles, the team conducted a SWOT analysis.

They identified their strengths, including a talented development team and a unique product concept. They also identified their weaknesses, including a lack of market research and limited funding. They identified opportunities such as increasing demand for their type of product and potential partnerships with larger companies. They also identified threats such as competing products and market saturation.

Using this information, the team developed a new go-to-market strategy that focused on a niche target market and a more compelling value proposition. They also prioritized market research and sought additional funding to support their efforts. The result was a more successful product launch that generated significant revenue and growth for the startup.

Identifying obstacles is an essential step in achieving success in personal and professional life. By using techniques such as process mapping, process review, soliciting feedback, SWOT analysis, and mind mapping, individuals and organizations can identify and overcome obstacles that are hindering their progress. Case studies have demonstrated that these techniques can be applied in a variety of contexts, from improving processes in a marketing department to developing a successful go-to-market strategy for a startup. By applying these techniques, individuals and organizations can achieve their goals and reach their full potential.

The Importance of Clear Communication and Accountability

Clear communication and accountability are crucial elements for identifying obstacles and solving problems effectively. Without these elements, it's challenging to identify and address the root causes of problems, and it's difficult to hold people accountable for their actions or inactions. In this section, we will discuss the importance of clear communication and accountability, how they can facilitate problem-solving, and how to implement them in personal and professional settings.

Clear Communication

Clear communication involves conveying information accurately and effectively to ensure that everyone understands what needs to be done, by whom, and when. It's a critical element in problem-solving, as it ensures that everyone is on the same page and working towards the same goals. Clear communication also fosters a sense of trust and transparency, which is essential for effective problem-solving.

Examples:

In a manufacturing company, the production manager communicates the daily production targets to the team clearly and effectively, along with the resources required to achieve the targets. This ensures that the team knows what is expected of them, and they can plan their work accordingly.

In a software development team, the project manager communicates the project goals and timelines to the team members clearly and regularly. This helps the team members understand their roles and responsibilities and enables them to collaborate effectively.

Accountability

Accountability refers to taking responsibility for one's actions or inactions and being answerable for the results. It's an essential element in problem-solving, as it ensures that individuals are held responsible for their actions and are incentivized to work towards achieving the goals. Accountability also fosters a culture of ownership and responsibility, which is crucial for effective problem-solving.

Examples:

In a sales team, the team leader holds team members accountable for their sales targets and regularly reviews their progress towards achieving them. This ensures that team members are motivated to work towards achieving the targets and are held responsible for their performance.

In a project management team, the project manager holds team members accountable for their deliverables and timelines. This ensures that team members take responsibility for their work and are incentivized to deliver high-quality work on time.

Implementing Clear Communication and Accountability

Implementing clear communication and accountability involves creating a culture of transparency, trust, and responsibility. This can be achieved by setting clear expectations, providing regular feedback, and fostering an environment of open communication. It's also essential to ensure that there are consequences for non-performance or non-compliance, and individuals are held accountable for their actions or inactions.

Case Study:

In a healthcare organization, the administration noticed that the patient waiting times were high, and patients were dissatisfied with the services. After conducting a root cause analysis, the administration identified that the communication between the front desk staff and the healthcare providers was poor, which led to delays in patient appointments. The administration implemented a communication and accountability plan, which included clear guidelines on how the front desk staff and healthcare providers should communicate, regular feedback on performance, and consequences for non-performance. The implementation of the plan led to a significant reduction in waiting times and improved patient satisfaction.

Clear communication and accountability are essential elements in problem-solving and efficiency. They ensure that everyone is working towards the same goals and that individuals are held responsible for their actions or inactions. By implementing clear communication and accountability in personal and professional settings, individuals and organizations can foster a culture of transparency, trust, and responsibility, which is crucial for effective problem-solving.

Assessing the Impact of Obstacles on Efficiency:

Identifying obstacles is an essential step in problem-solving, but it's equally important to assess their impact on efficiency. Assessing the impact of obstacles involves understanding how they affect processes, people, and resources, and how much they cost in terms of time, money, and effort. In this section, we will discuss the importance of assessing the impact of obstacles on efficiency, how to do it effectively, and how to use the results to make informed decisions.

Understanding the Impact of Obstacles

Understanding the impact of obstacles is crucial for effective problem-solving. Obstacles can have significant effects on processes, people, and resources, and it's essential to understand how they affect efficiency. By understanding the impact of obstacles, we can identify which obstacles are the most significant, prioritize them, and focus our efforts on addressing them.

Examples:

In a manufacturing company, a bottleneck in the production process can significantly impact efficiency, as it can lead to delays in production, increased costs, and decreased customer satisfaction.

In a customer service team, a lack of training can impact efficiency, as it can lead to long wait times, dissatisfied customers, and increased customer churn.

How to Assess the Impact of Obstacles

Assessing the impact of obstacles involves gathering data, analyzing it, and making informed decisions based on the results. The following steps can help assess the impact of obstacles effectively:

Identify the obstacle

The first step is to identify the obstacle that is causing the problem. This can be done through root cause analysis, process mapping, or other problem-solving techniques.

Gather data

The next step is to gather data on the obstacle, such as the frequency, duration, and impact on efficiency. This data can be gathered through surveys, interviews, or data analysis.

Analyze the data

Once the data is gathered, it's important to analyze it to understand the impact of the obstacle on efficiency. This can be done through statistical analysis, trend analysis, or other data analysis techniques.

Prioritize the obstacles

Based on the analysis, prioritize the obstacles that are having the most significant impact on efficiency. This will help to focus efforts on addressing the most critical obstacles.

Case Study

In a transportation company, the dispatch process was causing delays in delivery, increased costs, and decreased customer satisfaction. After conducting a root cause analysis, the company identified that the dispatch process was manual, which led to errors and delays. The company gathered data on the dispatch process, such as the frequency of errors, the time it took to dispatch trucks, and the impact on efficiency. The data analysis showed that the dispatch process was causing a significant impact on efficiency. The company prioritized the dispatch process as the most critical obstacle and implemented an automated dispatch system, which led to significant improvements in efficiency, reduced costs, and increased customer satisfaction.

Using the Results to Make Informed Decisions

Assessing the impact of obstacles on efficiency is essential for making informed decisions on how to address them. Once the impact of obstacles is understood, it's important to use the results to make data-driven decisions on how to improve efficiency. This may involve making changes to processes, investing in technology or equipment, or providing training to employees.

Examples:

In a retail store, the store manager may decide to invest in a new point-of-sale system to reduce wait times at checkout and improve customer satisfaction.

In a construction company, the project manager may decide to provide training to employees on safety procedures to reduce the number of accidents and improve efficiency.

Assessing the impact of obstacles on efficiency is an essential step in problem-solving. By understanding how obstacles affect processes, people, and resources, we can prioritize the most significant obstacles and focus our efforts on addressing them. Gathering data, analyzing it, and using the results to make informed decisions are critical to improving efficiency and achieving business goals. By making data-driven decisions, organizations can improve efficiency, reduce costs, and increase customer satisfaction.

Assessing the impact of obstacles on efficiency is not only critical to identifying problems but also to solving them. It provides valuable insights into how obstacles affect efficiency and helps to prioritize which obstacles to address first. By using data to make informed decisions, organizations can improve their processes, reduce costs, and increase customer satisfaction.

In the next chapter, we will discuss the importance of making tough decisions and strategies for dealing with difficult people or situations. By having the courage to make tough decisions, you can eliminate obstacles and streamline your processes, leading to greater efficiency and productivity.

Identifying obstacles and solving problems efficiently is essential for personal and professional growth. In this chapter, we discussed the importance of clear communication and accountability in identifying obstacles, assessing their impact on efficiency, and making informed decisions based on the results.

We highlighted how clear communication and accountability can help individuals and organizations work together towards common goals, and how they can foster a culture of trust, transparency, and responsibility. Clear communication ensures that everyone is working towards the same objectives, and accountability ensures that individuals are held responsible for their actions or inactions. Together, these two elements create a culture that promotes efficiency and problem-solving.

We also discussed how to assess the impact of obstacles on efficiency effectively. Understanding how obstacles affect processes, people, and resources is crucial for identifying which obstacles are the most significant, prioritizing them, and focusing efforts on addressing them. By gathering data, analyzing it, and making informed decisions based on the results, individuals and organizations can improve their processes, reduce costs, and increase customer satisfaction.

Furthermore, we provided examples and case studies that demonstrate how clear communication, accountability, and effective assessment of obstacles can contribute to personal and professional success. From a manufacturing company to a transportation company, the case studies show how identifying and addressing obstacles can have a significant impact on efficiency, customer satisfaction, and bottom-line results.

Subsequently, identifying obstacles and solving problems efficiently is crucial for personal and professional growth. Clear communication, accountability, and effective assessment of obstacles are critical elements that promote efficiency and problem-solving. By implementing these elements in personal and professional settings, individuals and organizations can foster a culture of trust, transparency, and responsibility that enables them to identify and address obstacles effectively. As a result, they can achieve their goals efficiently, reduce costs, and increase customer satisfaction.

Chapter 3

Making Tough Decisions

In life, we often face situations that require us to make tough decisions. Whether it's in our personal or professional lives, difficult decisions can be challenging to make, but they are often necessary for growth and success. Making tough decisions requires courage, clarity of thought, and the ability to consider the long-term benefits over short-term gains.

In this chapter, we will discuss the role of management in making tough decisions, strategies for dealing with difficult people or situations, and the importance of considering the long-term benefits of making tough decisions. We will also provide examples and case studies that demonstrate how effective decision-making can lead to personal and professional growth.

Making tough decisions can be particularly challenging in professional settings, where the stakes are high, and the consequences of poor decisions can be severe. Managers and leaders often have to make tough decisions that affect their teams, their organizations, and their customers. The ability to make tough decisions effectively is critical for achieving business goals, building strong relationships, and maintaining a healthy work environment.

In personal life, making tough decisions can be just as challenging, if not more so. It can involve anything from deciding to end a toxic relationship to making a significant career change. Making these decisions requires clarity of thought, emotional intelligence, and a willingness to take risks and step outside one's comfort zone.

In this chapter, we will discuss some of the strategies and techniques that can help individuals and organizations make tough decisions effectively. We will also provide examples and case studies that demonstrate the benefits of effective decision-making.

Making tough decisions is not easy, but it is an essential part of personal and professional growth. By learning to make tough decisions effectively, individuals and organizations can achieve their goals, build stronger relationships, and maintain a healthy work environment. The ability to make tough decisions is a valuable skill that can be developed over time through practice and experience.

The Role of Management in Making Tough Decisions

Making tough decisions can be challenging, and the role of management is crucial in guiding the decision-making process. Managers are responsible for identifying obstacles, assessing their impact on efficiency, and making tough decisions that will eliminate obstacles and improve processes. In this section, we will discuss the role of management in making tough decisions, and how managers can effectively navigate the decision-making process.

Role of Management:

Identifying obstacles

The first step in making tough decisions is identifying obstacles that are hindering efficiency. Managers play a critical role in identifying obstacles by analyzing processes, gathering data, and seeking feedback from employees and stakeholders.

Assessing impact

Once obstacles are identified, it's essential to assess their impact on efficiency. Managers must analyze data, identify trends, and determine the cost of obstacles in terms of time, money, and effort.

Weighing options

After identifying obstacles and assessing their impact, managers must weigh options and make tough decisions. They must consider short-term and long-term implications, risks, and benefits, and evaluate the feasibility and impact of each option.

Communicating decisions

Once tough decisions are made, managers must communicate them effectively to all stakeholders. They must explain the reasons behind the decision, the impact it will have, and how it aligns with the organization's goals.

Examples:

In a software development team, the project manager identified a lack of skills in the team that was hindering efficiency. The project manager assessed the impact of the lack of skills and identified that it was causing delays in the project and affecting customer satisfaction. The project manager made a tough decision to provide training to team members to improve their skills. The project manager communicated the decision to the team and explained the benefits of training, how it would impact the project, and how it aligned with the company's goals.

In a healthcare organization, the administration identified that outdated technology was hindering efficiency and causing delays in patient care. The administration assessed the impact of outdated technology and determined that it was affecting patient satisfaction, staff morale, and increasing costs. The administration made a tough decision to invest in new technology, which would improve patient care, reduce costs, and increase staff morale. The administration communicated the decision to stakeholders, explaining the reasons behind the decision, the benefits it would bring, and how it aligned with the organization's goals.

Effective Decision Making:

Effective decision-making is critical to solving problems and improving efficiency. Making tough decisions often requires collaboration, data-driven analysis, and careful consideration of risks and benefits. In this section, we will discuss the importance of effective decision-making, and how managers can use collaboration, data-driven analysis, balancing risks and benefits, and accountability to make tough decisions that improve efficiency.

Collaboration

Effective decision-making involves collaboration and input from all stakeholders. Collaboration ensures that decisions are informed by multiple perspectives, and stakeholders are invested in the outcomes. Managers must seek feedback and perspectives from employees, customers, and other stakeholders to make informed decisions.

Examples:

1. In a marketing team, the team leader may involve team members in decision-making processes by seeking feedback on campaigns and messaging. This can lead to more effective campaigns that resonate with the target audience.

2. In a healthcare organization, the administration may involve patients and their families in decision-making processes by seeking feedback on patient care and services. This can lead to improved patient satisfaction and better outcomes.

Collaboration can be facilitated through various techniques, such as brainstorming, focus groups, surveys, or stakeholder meetings. It's important to create an environment that fosters open communication and encourages participation from all stakeholders.

Data-Driven

Effective decision-making involves basing decisions on data and analysis rather than assumptions or opinions. Managers must gather data, analyze it, and make informed decisions based on the results. Data-driven decision-making provides an objective basis for decisions and reduces the risk of bias or subjective judgments.

Examples:

1. In a financial organization, the CEO may base decisions on financial data, such as revenue, expenses, and profitability. This can help to identify areas for improvement and guide strategic planning.

2. In a manufacturing company, the operations manager may base decisions on production data, such as efficiency, quality, and yield. This can help to identify bottlenecks and improve production processes.

Data can be gathered through various techniques, such as surveys, focus groups, or data analysis. It's important to ensure that data is reliable, relevant, and up-to-date.

Balancing Risks and Benefits

Effective decision-making involves considering the risks and benefits of each decision and weighing the short-term and long-term implications of each option. Managers must evaluate the potential risks and benefits of each decision and make informed judgments about the best course of action.

Examples:

1. In a technology company, the CEO may evaluate the risks and benefits of launching a new product. The CEO may consider the financial risks of investing in a new product, the potential benefits of increased revenue and market share, and the long-term implications of the decision.

2. In a healthcare organization, the administration may evaluate the risks and benefits of implementing new technology. The administration may consider the financial risks of investing in new technology, the potential benefits of improved patient care and reduced costs, and the long-term implications of the decision.

Balancing risks and benefits involves considering multiple factors, such as financial implications, market trends, customer needs, and long-term goals. It's important to weigh the potential risks and benefits of each decision objectively and make informed judgments.

Accountability

Effective decision-making involves taking responsibility for tough decisions and being accountable for their results. Managers must communicate decisions clearly, take action to ensure they are implemented effectively, and take responsibility for the outcomes.

Examples:

1. In a project management team, the team leader may communicate tough decisions about timelines and resources to team members clearly. The team leader may take responsibility for ensuring that the project is completed on time and within budget.

2. In a retail store, the store manager may communicate tough decisions about inventory management to employees clearly. The store manager may take responsibility for

Making tough decisions is essential for achieving business goals and improving efficiency. Managers play a crucial role in identifying obstacles, assessing their impact, weighing options, and communicating decisions effectively. Effective decision-making involves collaboration, data-driven analysis, balancing risks and benefits, and accountability. By making tough decisions and eliminating obstacles, organizations can improve their processes, reduce costs, and increase customer satisfaction.

Strategies for Dealing with Difficult People or Situations

Making tough decisions often involves dealing with difficult people or situations. These challenges can create stress, conflict, and uncertainty, making decision-making even more challenging. In this section, we will discuss strategies for dealing with difficult people or situations and how to navigate tough decisions effectively.

Active Listening

Active listening is a critical skill for dealing with difficult people or situations. Active listening involves paying attention to the speaker, clarifying what they are saying, and reflecting on their message. By actively listening, managers can gain a better understanding of the problem, identify underlying issues, and find common ground for solutions.

Examples:

In a team meeting, a team member may express frustration with a project's progress. The team leader may use active listening to understand the reasons for the frustration, identify any underlying issues, and find ways to address them.

In a customer service setting, a customer may express dissatisfaction with a product or service. The customer service representative may use active listening to understand the customer's concerns, offer solutions, and restore customer satisfaction.

Active listening can be facilitated through techniques such as paraphrasing, summarizing, and asking clarifying questions. It's important to create a safe and open environment that fosters active listening and encourages constructive dialogue.

Conflict Resolution

Dealing with difficult people or situations often involves managing conflict. Conflict can arise from differences in opinions, interests, or values, and can create tension, stress, and uncertainty. Conflict resolution involves identifying the source of the conflict, finding common ground, and developing solutions that satisfy all parties involved.

Examples:

In a team meeting, team members may have different opinions about the best approach to a project. The team leader may use conflict resolution techniques to identify the reasons for the different opinions, find common ground, and develop a solution that satisfies all team members.

In a customer service setting, a customer may have a dispute with a product or service. The customer service representative may use conflict resolution techniques to identify the reasons for the dispute, find common ground, and develop a solution that satisfies the customer.

Conflict resolution can be facilitated through techniques such as active listening, empathy, and compromise. It's important to establish clear communication and create a safe and open environment that fosters conflict resolution and encourages collaboration.

Assertiveness

Dealing with difficult people or situations often requires assertiveness. Assertiveness involves expressing opinions, needs, and feelings clearly and respectfully. By being assertive, managers can set boundaries, communicate expectations, and negotiate solutions effectively.

Examples:

In a team meeting, a team member may not be meeting project deadlines. The team leader may use assertiveness to communicate expectations, set clear deadlines, and ensure that the team member understands their responsibilities.

In a customer service setting, a customer may be demanding an unreasonable request. The customer service representative may use assertiveness to communicate company policies, explain why the request is unreasonable, and offer alternative solutions.

Assertiveness can be facilitated through techniques such as using "I" statements, expressing emotions clearly and respectfully, and setting clear boundaries. It's important to balance assertiveness with empathy and active listening to ensure effective communication and collaboration.

Dealing with difficult people or situations can create stress, conflict, and uncertainty, making decision-making even more challenging. However, by using strategies such as active listening, conflict resolution, and assertiveness, managers can navigate tough decisions effectively and find solutions that satisfy all parties involved. By creating a safe and open environment that fosters constructive dialogue and collaboration, managers can improve efficiency, reduce costs, and increase customer satisfaction.

Chapter 4

Cutting the String

This chapter is all about the several ways that we may remove the barriers that prevent us from reaching our objectives. There are times when the only way to get over these challenges is to force ourselves to make difficult choices and sever the ties that are holding us back. When it comes to letting go of things or people that are familiar to us, cutting the cord may be a challenging and unpleasant experience.

More attention will be paid to the process of cutting the string during the course of this chapter. In this chapter, you'll learn how to recognize strings that need to be severed, as well as the considerations that go into determining whether or not to severe a string, and the typical roadblocks that might appear in the way. In addition, we will discuss methods for successfully conveying difficult choices, which will include a discussion of how to approach the topic of discussion with stakeholders as well as pointers for handling opposition and reaction.

The act of cutting the string might be difficult, but it also presents a chance to get rid of the things that are preventing us from achieving our objectives and to make progress in that direction. Learning how to cut the rope efficiently will allow us to break free of the limitations imposed by the past and pave the way for a more promising future not just for ourselves but also for others around us. Therefore, without further ado, let us dive right in and go step by step through the process of cutting the string.

Identifying the Strings to Cut

Identifying the Strings that need to be cut

The process of overcoming challenges and accomplishing our objectives involves a number of steps, one of which is the determination of which strings need to be severed. Everything that impedes our progress or keeps us from going ahead is referred to be a string. Bad habits, toxic relationships, outmoded ideas, and fruitless hobbies are just a few examples of the strings that may be pulled. To be able to cut these strings, you must first have a solid comprehension of what they are and how they influence our life. In this part of the chapter, we will discuss how to recognize strings that need to be severed.

Conduct a Self-Assessment

Doing an honest evaluation of oneself is the first step that has to be taken in order to determine which strings need to be severed. This entails taking a critical look at your life and pinpointing the areas in which you feel held back or trapped. Examine your long-term objectives, core principles, and top priorities in light of the circumstances you find yourself in right now. Ask yourself questions like:

- What do I want to accomplish throughout the course of my life?
- Where do I stand with regard to the most difficult problems or difficulties?
- Which of my pursuits or relationships are consuming the most of my time and energy?
- Which of my routines or ways of acting do I wish to alter?

If you answer these questions in an honest manner, you will be able to obtain a better understanding of the strings that may be holding you back.

Analyze Your Environment

Doing an analysis of your surroundings is yet another method for locating strings that need to be severed. This encompasses both the physical environment (such as your job, residence, or social situations) and the social environment (e.g. the people you spend time with or the media you consume). Consider the following inquiries:

- Which components of my surroundings cause me the most anxiety or are the most distracting?

- Who are the individuals in my life who encourage and uplift me, and who saps my strength and vitality?

- What kinds of media and social networks do I often utilize, and how do they affect my mood or my ability to get things done?

- How does the state of my physical surroundings affect my ability to concentrate and stay motivated? Is it messy or disorganized?

You may find strings that may be holding you back by doing an analysis of your surroundings and then beginning to make adjustments that will support the objectives you have set for yourself.

Examine Your Mindset and Beliefs

The way we think and the ideas we have may sometimes act as shackles that prevent us from moving forward. Both our self-confidence and our drive may suffer when we engage in self-defeating behaviors such as negative self-talk, limiting beliefs, and self-doubt. Asking yourself the following questions can help you find strings associated with your thinking and beliefs:

- What beliefs do I have about myself or my talents that might be preventing me from reaching my full potential?
- How does the way I speak to myself effect my confidence and motivation?
- What worries or concerns do I have that might be preventing me from moving forward?

You may start to confront the negative ideas and beliefs that may be holding you back by beginning to examine your mentality and beliefs. This will allow you to establish a mindset that is more positive and powerful for you.

Look for Patterns

Lastly, in order to determine which strings need to be severed, it is essential to search for patterns in either your conduct or your surroundings. For instance, if you discover that you procrastinate on a regular basis or that it is difficult for you to maintain a good work-life balance, these might be indications that you need to cut some strings in terms of how you handle your time or how productive you are. If you discover that you are in a relationship with someone who is consistently negative or poisonous, this may be a clue that you need to sever some of the strings that are connected to that connection or adjust your boundaries.

You may find strings that may be holding you back by searching for patterns in your behavior or surroundings. After you have identified these strings, you can begin to make adjustments to better your position.

Subsequently, one of the most important steps in the process of overcoming challenges and accomplishing objectives is to identify the strings that need to be severed. You can gain a clearer picture of what strings may be holding you back and begin to make changes that will support your success by conducting a self-assessment, analyzing your environment, examining your mindset and beliefs, and looking for patterns. By doing all of these things, you will be able to find patterns.

Factors to Consider when Making a Decision to Cut a String

Eliminating roadblocks and releasing ourselves from everything that keeps us back is the act of cutting the string. When we have to let go of things or people who are familiar to us, it may be tough and painful to cut the string. For our own development, enjoyment, and success, however, it is often essential to cut the string. In this part of the discussion, we will investigate the reasons for the need of severing the string at times.

Overcoming Fear and Resistance

The need to conquer anxiety and reluctance is one of the primary drivers behind the sometimes pressing need to sever the string. When we are fearful of the unknown or uncomfortable with change, we often cling to things that are familiar to us, even if they are no longer useful to us. Cutting the string demands bravery as well as the determination to confront our concerns and move beyond them.

Cutting the string, for instance, may force you to address your fears of being alone or of the unknown if you are in a toxic relationship that saps your energy and leaves you feeling sad. Due to the fact that transitioning into anything new may be challenging and unpleasant, it may be necessary for you to overcome any resistance shown by the other person or even from inside yourself.

You can conquer your anxieties and overcome your reluctance by cutting the string, which will also provide room for new

Eliminating Negative Influences

Cutting the string is also important in order to free our life from the influence of destructive outside forces. Negative influences may take many different forms, including poisonous relationships, unhealthy habits, or restricting ideas. These factors may prevent us from accomplishing our objectives and leading the life we envision for ourselves.

For instance, if you have a terrible tendency of putting things off until later, cutting the string can require you to give up diversions or time-wasting hobbies that support that behavior. Cutting the string may require you to restrict or discontinue a connection with a friend or family member who consistently undermines or belittles you.

You may build a more positive and supportive atmosphere for yourself that enables you to grow if you get rid of the negative influences in your life.

Creating Space for Growth

Cutting the string is also important in order to make room for development and new possibilities. When we cling to things that are no longer beneficial to us, we restrict our potential and prevent ourselves from experiencing new things.

For instance, if you are clinging to a job that no longer challenges or satisfies you, cutting the string may require you to resign from that position in order to free up space in your schedule for other potential career paths. Cutting the string may force you to question and modify a belief that you have been clinging to for too long even though it is no longer serving you.

You may expose yourself to new experiences, new points of view, and new opportunities if you make room for development in your life.

Achieving Your Goals

In the end, you will need to sever the string in order to accomplish what you set out to do. When we cling to things that aren't in our best interests, we restrict our potential and make it more difficult to accomplish our objectives.

If you want to establish your own company, for instance, cutting the string could force you to give up the comfort and security of your present position and take a chance on your entrepreneurial endeavor. Cutting the string may require you to let rid of harmful habits or relationships that undermine your development if your objective is to enhance your health and fitness.

We may improve our chances of achieving our objectives by severing the string that binds us and doing away with the obstacles that stand in the way of our progress toward those objectives.

Subsequently, cutting the string is sometimes required to overcome fear and reluctance, remove harmful influences, create room for development, and realize our objectives. Cutting the string might be challenging and painful; but, it is frequently important for our personal development, happiness, and success. We may create a better future for ourselves and people around us by being ready to let go of things that are no longer beneficial to us.

Common Obstacles to Cutting the String

Cutting the string may be a trying process, and there are numerous roadblocks that can make it difficult to let go of things that are no longer serving their purpose for us. Emotional relationships and the fear of the unknown are two examples of these types of roadblocks. In this part, we'll discuss some of the more typical challenges that people have while trying to cut the string, as well as some strategies for overcoming those challenges.

Emotional Attachments

Emotional attachments are one of the most typical types of roadblocks that prevent people from severing the string. We often cling to objects or people because we have an emotional connection to them. When there are strong feelings involved, it might be difficult to let go of anything, whether it's a treasured possession, a cherished animal, or a close friend.

To be successful in overcoming this barrier, it is necessary to acknowledge the fact that emotional attachments have the potential to inhibit both our personal development and our level of enjoyment. Even while it's normal to form ties to the people and things in our lives, it's essential to be able to identify when those connections are no longer beneficial to us. We may begin to change our viewpoint and overcome emotional attachments by concentrating on the possible advantages of letting go, such as making room for new experiences and possibilities.

Fear of the Unknown

Fear of the unknown is yet another prevalent barrier that prevents people from cutting the string. When we let go of something, we often enter a period of time in which the future and its results are unclear to us. Especially if we're used to a specific habit or surroundings, this might be frightening and unpleasant.

It is crucial to acknowledge that change is a necessary aspect of both our personal development and the accomplishment of our objectives in order to be successful in overcoming this challenge. While venturing into the unknown might be nerve-wracking at times, doing so presents a chance for personal development and growth. We may start to change our viewpoint and get over our fear of the unknown if we concentrate on the possible rewards of taking risks, such as earning new abilities or experiences.

Social Pressure

Another barrier to cutting the string is social pressure. Friends, family, or even society at large may put pressure on us to maintain particular relationships or routines, even if they are no longer in our best interests. Because of this pressure, it may be difficult for us to break free and follow our own objectives and aspirations.

To be successful in overcoming this challenge, it is essential to acknowledge that our own personal development and contentment should be our highest priorities. While it is necessary to take into account the perspectives of other people, in the end, we are the ones who will be the ones to bear the repercussions of the choices we make. We may start to resist societal pressure and cut the string by being loyal to our own beliefs and objectives.

Habitual Patterns

Another typical barrier to severing the string is habitual routines. Even if we are aware that some patterns or behaviors are no longer beneficial to us, it may be difficult for us to break free of them. This may be a particularly difficult task if the habits in question have been acquired over an extended period of time.

It is crucial to know that habits may be altered with time and effort, which is the first step in overcoming this difficulty. We may start to break away from old patterns and make progress toward a life that is more rewarding if we establish new objectives for ourselves and adopt new habits. It is essential to keep in mind that making changes requires time and work, thus it is necessary to exercise patience and perseverance in your attempts to cut the string.

Financial Worries

Another barrier to breaking the string is financial worries. Even if a job or source of money is not enjoyable or in line with our objectives, we may be reluctant to let up of it. Having dependents or other financial commitments might make this a particularly difficult task to do.

To be successful in overcoming this barrier, it is essential to acknowledge the fact that monetary problems may be resolved by careful planning and organization. We may begin to take steps toward a professional path that is more rewarding and consistent with our values and interests by establishing financial objectives and developing a budget. To ensure that we are able to sustain ourselves financially while working toward our objectives, it is essential that we investigate potential additional income streams, such as freelancing or a second job.

Cutting the String

Strategies for Cutting the String Effectively

Cutting the string is the process of letting go of things that are no longer beneficial to us, whether they be relationships, habits, or beliefs. Cutting the string is a vital procedure for both personal development and the accomplishment of our objectives, despite the fact that it may be a challenging task. In the following paragraphs, we will discuss several methods that may be used to efficiently cut the string.

Identify What Needs to Be Cut

Finding out what has to be cut is the first step in cutting the string. This may need you to examine your relationships, routines, and beliefs to figure out what aspects of your life are no longer beneficial to you. When you have determined what can be eliminated, the next step is to examine the reasons behind your decision to do so in an open and forthright manner. This might assist you in maintaining your motivation and dedication to the procedure.

Visualize Your Ideal Outcome

When you have determined what has to be eliminated, it might be beneficial to picture the final product as you would want it to be. Imagine what your life would be like after you have let go of the things that are no longer beneficial to you. You may keep yourself motivated and focused on your objectives by envisioning the result that you want.

Set Clear Boundaries

Cutting the string successfully requires the establishment of distinct boundaries. This may include explaining your choice to others around you and establishing distinct boundaries between what you will and will not put up with. You may safeguard yourself against detrimental influences and maintain your dedication to your objectives if you establish distinct limits.

Develop a Support System

For cutting the string efficiently, a support system must be developed. This may include requesting assistance from friends, family, or a therapist to help you get through the process. In addition, while you work toward achieving your objectives, having a support system may assist you in remaining responsible and motivated.

Practice Self-Care

While cutting the string, it is essential to engage in self-care practices. Taking care of your mental and physical health by engaging in activities such as exercise, meditation, and therapy are all examples of what this might entail. Even when the process seems difficult, it may be helpful to keep grounded and focused on your objectives if you engage in self-care practices regularly.

Be Patient and Persistent

It takes time and effort to cut the string. While you work toward achieving your objectives, it is essential to have a patient and dogged attitude. This may be accomplished by establishing a series of smaller milestones and celebrating each one along the way. You may maintain your motivation and dedication to your objectives by being patient and persistent.

Learn from Your Experience

Last but not least, when it comes to cutting the string, it is essential to gain knowledge from experience. As part of this process, you may consider what aspects of your strategy went well and which did not, and then make adjustments based on what you learn from this analysis as you go ahead. You may continue to develop and progress as a person by gaining new knowledge from your experiences and using that knowledge.

Subsequently, severing the string might be a difficult procedure, but it is essential for our personal development and the accomplishment of our objectives. Identifying what needs to be cut, picturing your ultimate result, establishing clear limits, building a support system, practicing self-care, being patient and persistent, and learning from your experience are all helpful strategies for cutting the string. If you effectively implement these tactics into your approach, you will be able to successfully cut the string and establish a life that is more rewarding for you.

Tips for Communicating Tough Decisions to Others

It may be difficult to communicate difficult choices to others, particularly when such decisions include severing the string and letting go of connections, habits, or beliefs. In the following paragraphs, we will discuss several useful strategies for successfully expressing difficult judgments.

Be Clear and Direct

It is crucial to be as straightforward and direct as possible while explaining difficult choices to others. This requires you to convey your judgment and the rationale behind it in a manner that is straightforward and succinct. If you want to avoid uncertainty and misunderstanding, you should steer clear of tactics such as "beating about the bush" and "sugarcoating" your message.

Utilize "I" Statements

It is possible to express difficult judgments without assigning blame or inciting defensiveness by making use of "I" statements, which is a successful method. Try replacing the phrase "you are the reason I need to sever connections" with "I have chosen to cut ties for my own personal development." This strategy may make the other person feel less assaulted, which will increase the likelihood that they will accept your choice.

Avoid Criticism and Judgment

When expressing difficult choices, it is critical to avoid criticism and judgment as much as possible. Instead of concentrating on what the other person did incorrectly, you should think on the reasons why you need to make the choice for your own personal development. Critique and judgment might make the other person defensive and less inclined to accept your choice.

Listen to the Other Person

When expressing difficult choices, it is vital to be clear and straightforward, but it is also important to listen to the other person. Both of these things are equally important. This might include paying attention to their point of view and recognizing the emotions that they are experiencing. Even if you don't share their viewpoint, just making the effort to hear what they have to say might make them feel heard and valued.

Provide a Clear Reason for Your Decision

If you explain to the other person why you have made the choice that you have made, they may find it easier to accept it and comprehend it. This might include discussing why the choice is vital for your own development and how it will benefit both you and the other person in the long run. If you provide the other person with a clear explanation for your decision, it may assist them feel more inclined to support your choice.

Offer Support

By showing support, you may make the other person feel less alone, which in turn increases the likelihood that they will accept your choice. This might include offering to keep in contact, giving resources for help, or just being there to listen if they need to chat. Even though the choice is challenging, showing support for the other person may help keep the relationship pleasant.

Follow Through on Your Decision

When it comes to conveying difficult choices to others, one last thing to keep in mind is how crucial it is to stick to your decision. This implies that you must remain steadfast in your choice and not give the other person the power to sway you in any way. The other person may find it easier to accept your choice and go on with their life if you stick to your decision and carry it out.

Subsequently, conveying difficult choices to others might be difficult, but there are effective techniques for doing so. Being clear and straightforward, utilizing "I" statements, avoiding criticism and judgment, listening to the other person, giving a clear justification for your choice, showing support, and following through on your decision are all helpful hints for successfully communicating difficult decisions. You will be able to convey difficult choices in a manner that is both courteous and productive if you include these guidelines into your strategy.

Approaching the Conversation with Stakeholders

It is very uncommon to feel intimidated while approaching a meeting with stakeholders, particularly when the talk may include making difficult choices that will affect them. In this part, we will discuss ways for addressing the dialogue with stakeholders in a manner that is both successful and courteous.

Make preparations in advance

It is essential that preparation be completed in advance before entering the dialogue with the stakeholders. This might include doing research on the viewpoints of the stakeholders, preparing for the possibility of questions or concerns being raised, and formulating essential topics to discuss during the talk. You will be able to feel more assured and guarantee that the discussion continues on its intended path if you prepare in advance.

Set the Stage

The first step in approaching the dialogue with stakeholders is to establish the context for the discussion. This may include arranging the meeting in advance, establishing a definite agenda for the chat, and creating an atmosphere that is both comfortable and courteous for the dialogue to take place in. You may develop a feeling of trust and professionalism by setting the scene, which can make the dialogue more productive.

Be Honest and Transparent

It is essential to have an open and honest discussion about the matter with the various parties involved before beginning the dialogue. This necessitates being forthright about the choice that has to be taken as well as the factors that led to its need. Avoid painting a rosy picture of the circumstances or trying to hide behind ambiguous language since doing so might result in misunderstanding and distrust.

Listen to Stakeholders' Perspectives

Before beginning a dialogue with stakeholders, it is critical to first listen to their opinions. This may be done by attentively listening to their worries, recognizing the sensations they are experiencing, and responding to any questions or objections they may have. You can show the viewpoints of the stakeholders that their thoughts are valued, as well as assist them feel heard and appreciated, if you listen to what they have to say.

Focus on Solutions

Approaching the dialogue with the stakeholders in such a manner that the focus is on potential solutions is a productive method to go. Focusing on solutions that can handle the issue in a constructive manner rather than concentrating on the problem or what can't be done is a better course of action. This may include coming up with potential other solutions or looking for methods to lessen the impact of the choice.

Maintain Professionalism

While addressing the interaction with stakeholders, it is essential to keep one's professionalism intact. This requires refraining from making personal attacks or displaying strong emotions, and instead speaking in a way that is straightforward and courteous. You can assist the discussion remain on topic and avoid causing extra stress or disagreement if you keep a professional demeanor throughout the exchange.

Follow Up and Follow Through

After the interaction with stakeholders, it is critical to follow up with them and ensure that their concerns are addressed. Providing updates on the decision or its ramifications, as well as following through on any promises made during the talk, are both examples of what this might include. You may maintain a healthy connection with stakeholders if you follow up with them and show that you are committed to finding a solution that works for everyone by following through on what you say you will do.

Subsequently, initiating a dialogue with stakeholders might be difficult, but there are successful techniques for doing so. Preparing in preparation, creating the scene, being honest and upfront, listening to stakeholders' viewpoints, concentrating on solutions, retaining professionalism, and following up and following through are all helpful tips for conducting the dialogue with stakeholders successfully. You may have a dialogue with stakeholders that is courteous and productive if you follow the advice in this section and include it into your strategy.

Dealing with Resistance and Backlash

Cutting the string involves dealing with resistance and blowback. When difficult choices that have an impact on stakeholders are made, it is not uncommon for there to be opposition and backlash in reaction to such decisions. In this part of the chapter we will discuss some of the frequent responses that people have when the string is cut, as well as some tactics for dealing with resistance and backlash in a way that is productive and efficient.

Common Reactions to Cutting the String

Cutting the string may be a tough choice, and it is crucial to remember that stakeholders may have similar responses to the decision. In this section, we will discuss some of the most frequent responses that may take place while cutting the string, as well as some efficient ways to deal with these reactions after they have taken place.

Denial

Denial is a frequent response to severing the string. The use of denial as a defensive strategy is one way to protect oneself from having to confront the truth of the matter. The gravity of the problem or the need of the choice may be disputed by stakeholders. For instance, workers may argue that there is no need for layoffs, even though the firm is experiencing significant financial difficulties.

It is essential to express the judgment in an open and transparent manner in order to manage denial in an effective manner. Provide the people affected by the decision specific facts and examples of why the choice was taken, and explain how it will benefit the company in the long term. Try to comprehend why stakeholders may be in denial while exercising patience and empathy. You may assist to create trust and understanding by addressing their worries and feelings.

Anger

Anger is a frequent response to severing the string. Stakeholders may experience feelings of frustration, anger, or even betrayal as a result of the choice. One possible cause of this is the individual's perception that they were not consulted or involved in the decision-making process. For instance, if a corporation announces a merger that would lead to layoffs, workers may feel unhappy if they were not given a chance to weigh in on the decision.

Even if you don't share their sentiments, it's critical to show that you understand the feelings of those involved in the conflict and validate their experiences in order to properly manage their anger. In addition to this, it is essential to convey the choice in a way that is both clear and open to stakeholders, as well as to pay attention to their concerns and comments. You may help to create trust and understanding with them if you acknowledge their feelings and worries, and you can also help to reduce the likelihood that they will resist or retaliate against you.

Resistance

Another typical response to severing the string is resistance. Stakeholders may actively oppose the conclusion by refusing to participate or even undermining the process. This may be due to the individual believing that they have no control over the circumstance or that the choice is unjust. For instance, if a corporation introduces a new policy that workers feel strongly against, they may choose to resist the regulation by either actively speaking out against it or by simply not adhering to it.

It is essential to convey the decision in a way that is both clear and transparent, as well as to address the concerns and objections raised by stakeholders. Only then can resistance be properly managed. Also, it is essential to provide assistance and resources to stakeholders who may be affected in some way as a result of the decision. You may assist to reduce the likelihood of opposition by working together with stakeholders and resolving their concerns. This will also contribute to the development of trust and an increased level of comprehension.

Fear

When the string is severed, many people experience fear as a frequent response. There is a possibility that stakeholders would experience anxiety due to their fear of the unknown or the possible adverse effects of the decision. This may happen when people feel that their way of life or their sense of security is under jeopardy. Employees may be concerned about losing their employment, for instance, if a firm announces a merger that might lead to layoffs.

In order to successfully manage fear, it is essential to explain the decision in a manner that is both clear and transparent, as well as to give assistance and resources to stakeholders who may be affected in some way by the choice. It is also essential to address the concerns and objections raised by stakeholders, as well as to demonstrate empathy and patience while doing so. You may assist to reduce some of the bad impacts of the choice by offering support and addressing concerns. In doing so, you can also contribute to the building of trust and understanding.

Subsequently, frequent responses to severing the string include denial, anger, resistance, and terror. In order to handle these reactions effectively, it is important to communicate the decision in a clear and transparent manner, acknowledge the emotions and concerns of stakeholders, provide support and resources, address concerns and objections, be flexible, and keep one's focus on the bigger picture. You may assist to lessen any opposition and create trust and understanding among stakeholders by adding these methods into your strategy.

Strategies for Managing Resistance and Backlash

When faced with challenging choices that require one to "cut the string," it is critical to ensure that one is well-prepared for the possibility of opposition and blowback from various stakeholders. When opposition and backlash are successfully managed, it is possible to increase the likelihood that the decision will be carried out without incident and that the organization will be able to proceed without unneeded disturbance or conflict. In the following paragraphs, we will discuss various tactics that may be used to effectively manage opposition and backlash.

Communicate clearly and transparently

The ability to communicate in a way that is both clear and open is essential for effectively handling opposition and reaction. It is essential to have a transparent discussion on the choice, the thinking that went into it, as well as the possible effects on the various stakeholders. Provide specific examples and data to back up your conclusion, and don't be afraid to discuss any possible disadvantages or unfavorable outcomes in an open and forthright manner.

When it comes to the decision-making process itself, transparency is also a very significant factor. When it's feasible to do so, include stakeholders in the decision-making process and make sure they have plenty of chances to give feedback and input. This may serve to lessen the possibility for resistance and reaction, as well as contribute to the building of trust and understanding.

Empathize with stakeholders

When it comes to effectively handling opposition and backlash, empathy is a crucial talent to have. While addressing these issues, it is essential to have patience and empathy, as well as an awareness of the feelings and worries of those who have an interest in the matter. Even if you disagree with the feelings and worries that the stakeholders are expressing, it is important to acknowledge them and make an effort to put yourself in their position.

You can help to create trust and understanding among stakeholders, and you can help to lessen any opposition and backlash, all by demonstrating empathy and understanding.

Address concerns and objections

When several parties have issues or objections to a decision, it is essential to address these concerns head-on while maintaining a courteous demeanor. Spend some time actively listening to the comments and concerns expressed by stakeholders, and make an effort to comprehend their point of view. Address their concerns in a way that is both transparent and empathic, and provide tangible answers or other options whenever it is practicable to do so.

You can help to create trust and understanding among stakeholders if you address their worries and objections, and you can also assist to lessen the likelihood of resistance and backlash if you do so.

Provide support and resources

It is crucial to give assistance and resources to stakeholders who may be affected by a choice that entails cutting the string when the decision may have an effect on such stakeholders. This could take the form of counseling or coaching services, chances to gain new skills or update existing ones, or financial assistance.

You may assist to lessen the negative effect of the decision on stakeholders by giving support and resources, which can also contribute to the building of trust and an understanding of the situation.

Stay focused on the bigger picture

To effectively manage opposition and backlash, it is critical to maintain a focus on the greater goal at all times. Keep in mind the long-term objectives and values of the company, as well as the reason the choice was taken in the first place, and remember why it was made. While putting the choice into action, maintain patience and tenacity, and do not allow yourself to be derailed by temporary obstacles or disagreements.

You can assist guarantee that the organization remains on track and goes ahead efficiently even in the face of opposition and backlash if you keep your attention on the greater vision and do your best to maintain focus on that.

Be flexible

Last but not least, when it comes to dealing with opposition and backlash, it is essential to be adaptable. Have a receptive attitude toward comments and criticism, and be ready to make course corrections as required. Think about potential other solutions or concessions that could be better received by the stakeholders, and be open to make adjustments as necessary.

You can help to create trust and understanding with stakeholders if you are flexible and adaptive, and you can also assist to limit the possibility of opposition and backlash if you do so.

To summarize, effectively managing resistance and backlash requires clear and transparent communication, empathy, addressing concerns and objections, providing support and resources, remaining focused on the bigger picture, and being flexible. Additionally, it is necessary to stay focused on the bigger picture. You can assist to reduce the likelihood of possible opposition and establish trust and understanding among stakeholders if you include these methods into your strategy.

Handling Negative Feedback

When it comes to putting difficult choices into action, such as cutting the string, one of the most difficult aspects might be managing negative feedback or opposition. When several stakeholders voice their disagreement with a decision, it may be challenging to determine how to react in a manner that does not compromise the validity of the choice while at the same time addressing the concerns of the various stakeholders. In the following paragraphs, we will discuss various approaches that may be used when dealing successfully with unfavorable comments or pushback.

Listen actively

It is important to maintain an active and attentive listening posture in the event that stakeholders express unfavorable input or pushback. Active listening requires giving the person who is speaking your whole attention, asking questions that will help you better comprehend what they are saying, and restating what they have said in your own words to ensure that you have grasped their point of view.

You may show that you appreciate the thoughts and concerns of stakeholders by actively listening to them, which can also assist establish trust and understanding amongst the parties involved.

Acknowledge stakeholders' concerns

When it comes to dealing with unfavorable criticism or pushback, one of the most crucial things to do is acknowledge the concerns of stakeholders. You may display empathy and understanding by recognizing the worries of the stakeholders, which can also contribute to the development of trust and rapport.

When addressing the issues raised by stakeholders, it is critical to do so in a genuine and detailed manner. Try expressing your understanding by saying things like "I can see why that might be a worry for you" or "I see why you could feel that way." This may serve to legitimize the sentiments and worries of the stakeholders, which can contribute to a de-escalation of the issue.

Stay calm and professional

It is imperative that one maintains composure and a professional demeanor in the face of unfavorable comments or opposition. Averting yourself from being defensive or emotional is important if you want to prevent the problem from becoming even more difficult to settle.

Instead, maintain composure and concentrate on the task at hand while responding to the concerns of stakeholders in a way that is both professional and courteous. Maintain a level tone and steer clear of making any personal attacks or using language that might inflame the situation.

Provide additional information or clarification

It's possible that stakeholders won't offer positive feedback or pushback in some situations because they don't completely comprehend the choice or the logic that went into making it. Addressing these issues and helping to establish awareness and buy-in may be facilitated by providing extra information or explanation, respectively.

Be as clear and concrete as possible if you are offering more information or explanation. Make sure that any claims you make are backed up by facts and proof, and steer clear of using jargon or language that is too technical, since this might make it difficult for stakeholders to follow what you are saying.

Consider alternative solutions or compromises

When confronted with unfavorable criticism or pushback, it is possible that it will be essential to examine alternate options or compromises that satisfy the concerns of stakeholders while still fulfilling the aims of the decision. This may aid to contribute to the development of trust and comprehension among stakeholders, in addition to contributing to the upkeep of the decision's integrity.

Be innovative and open to new ideas while thinking about potential alternative solutions or compromises. Search for alternatives that will provide you the same results as the initial choice, but which will perhaps go down better with the various stakeholders.

Follow up and follow through

In the end, one of the most essential things to remember when dealing with unfavorable criticism or pushback is to make sure that any obligations or promises that were made to stakeholders are kept. It is possible that doing so will help to develop trust and credibility, as well as assist in maintaining strong relationships with stakeholders.

After the first chat, it is important to follow up with the various stakeholders involved to check in on their concerns and offer updates on the decision as well as any prospective modifications. Stick to your word and fulfill any pledges or promises you've made, such as giving further information or resources or taking into consideration other options for resolving a problem.

Subsequently, effectively handling negative feedback or pushback requires active listening, acknowledging the concerns of stakeholders, maintaining composure and maintaining a professional demeanor, providing additional information or clarification, considering alternative solutions or compromises, following up and following through, and so on. You may assist to create trust and understanding among stakeholders by integrating these tactics into your approach, and you can manage possible disputes and issues with more ease.

Moving Forward

Strategies for Moving Forward after Cutting the String

After severing the connection and addressing any opposition or blowback that may have resulted, the next step is to concentrate on going ahead and carrying out the decision in the most efficient manner possible. After the cutting of the thread, in this part we will discuss various techniques for going ahead and ensuring that the choice is effectively executed so that we may move on to the next stage.

Develop a clear plan of action

It is essential to design a distinct plan of action that describes the actions that need to be followed in order to put the choice into action in order to successfully go ahead after cutting the thread. Only then will it be possible to move forward in an effective manner. This strategy has to be detailed, attainable, and quantifiable. Moreover, it needs to contain explicit schedules and due dates for each stage.

You can guarantee that everyone engaged in the process of implementation is on the same page and knows what must be done if you prepare a detailed plan of action. This will allow you to ensure that the implementation process is successful. This may assist to guarantee that there is as little uncertainty as possible and that the decision is carried out in an effective and timely manner.

Communicate the plan effectively

When you have produced a detailed plan of action, it is essential to properly communicate that plan to all of the stakeholders who will be engaged in the process of putting the plan into action. This may involve customers, suppliers, or other external stakeholders in addition to staff.

When conveying the strategy to stakeholders, it is critical to do so in a way that is both clear and succinct, and to avoid using jargon or other technical terminology that may be difficult for them to grasp. In order to better show the strategy and make it simpler to comprehend, you may make use of visual aids such as flowcharts and timelines.

Assign responsibilities and accountability

It is necessary to assign duties and responsibility for each phase of the process in order to guarantee that the action plan will be carried out in the most efficient manner possible. This may entail allocating work to certain people or departments, or selecting external partners who will be accountable for certain portions of the implementation. Both of these options are viable options.

You can guarantee that everyone engaged in the process of implementation is aware of what it is that they are responsible for and understands the repercussions of failing to fulfill their commitments if you assign responsibilities and hold people accountable for their actions. This may assist to guarantee that the decision is effectively executed as well as the procedure that is being used to implement it remains on track.

Monitor progress and adjust as necessary

It is essential to keep track of progress over the course of the implementation process and make any required adjustments to the action plan. This may entail detecting impediments or issues that develop throughout the process of implementation, and altering the strategy in order to handle those challenges after they have been identified.

You can guarantee that the process of implementation remains on track and that the decision is effectively executed if you monitor the progress being made and make any required adjustments to the plan.

Celebrate successes and learn from failures

At the end of the process of implementation, it is essential to reflect on both the accomplishments that have been achieved and the mistakes that have been made. This may serve to boost morale and keep staff motivated, and it can also assist to uncover areas that might need improvement in the way future decisions are made.

While commemorating victories, it is important to be clear and concrete about the accomplishments that have been done, and it is also important to highlight the efforts of particular workers or departments. While trying to learn from past mistakes, it is important to be open and honest about the areas in which the implementation process fell short. Moreover, it is important to pinpoint the particular actions that can be done to ensure that similar errors are not made in the future.

To summarize, moving forward after cutting the string requires developing a clear plan of action, effectively communicating that plan, assigning responsibilities and accountability, monitoring progress and adjusting as necessary, celebrating successes and learning from failures. In addition, moving forward after cutting the string requires celebrating successes and learning from failures. You will be able to guarantee that the choice will be effectively executed and that the company will be able to reach its objectives in a manner that is both easier and more efficient if you include these methods into your approach.

Importance of Staying Focused on Goals

Maintaining one's attention on one's objectives is essential to achieving success in any endeavor, whether it professional or personal. Whether you're an individual working towards personal goals or a team working towards organizational objectives, maintaining focus on your goals is very necessary in order to accomplish what you set out to do and get the results you want. In the following section, we will discuss the significance of maintaining focus on objectives as well as several ways for doing so successfully.

Provides clarity and direction

Keeping one's attention on one's objectives helps both the person and the organization with clarity and direction. It is much simpler to determine the steps that need to be followed in order to reach one's aims and goals if one has clear objectives and goals. This clarity and direction not only helps people and teams remain focused and motivated, but it also guarantees that efforts are directed towards accomplishing the results that were sought.

Helps maintain motivation and momentum

While working toward long-term objectives, it is not uncommon to have hurdles or setbacks that may be discouraging to one's progress. These can be avoided, though. Even in the face of obstacles, individuals and teams may keep their motivation and momentum up by ensuring that they do not lose sight of the ultimate objective.

Individuals and teams are able to preserve a positive mindset and continue working toward the results they seek if they remember to constantly bring the ultimate goal into their thoughts. This is something that might be especially crucial to keep in mind during difficult times, when it can be easy to give up or grow disheartened.

Increases efficiency and effectiveness

Keeping one's attention on one's objectives may also help to boost one's effectiveness and efficiency. When people and teams have a crystal clear understanding of their aims and objectives, they are better able to prioritize their work and distribute their resources efficiently. This makes it easier to avoid spending time or money on activities that do not contribute to the accomplishment of the goals that have been set.

Individuals and teams may avoid distractions that might derail their efforts if they keep their concentration on the objectives they have set for themselves. This may be of utmost significance in the current world, which is characterized by a high rate of change and rapid speed, as well as an abundance of competing demands and diversions fighting for one's attention.

Provides a sense of accomplishment and fulfillment

Getting things done that you've set out to do may give you a feeling of success and satisfaction, both of which can be quite fulfilling. Individuals and teams may feel a sense of success and accomplishment while they work toward the results they seek if they keep their attention on the objectives they have set for themselves.

This feeling of success may serve to enhance morale and motivation, and it can also create a powerful sense of purpose and meaning. Also, it may assist in the development of confidence as well as resilience, both of which can be useful in both personal and professional settings.

Strategies for Staying Focused on Goals

Set SMART goals

Individuals and teams may benefit from staying focused on their goals by setting SMART goals, which are goals that are specific, measurable, attainable, relevant, and time-bound. The use of SMART objectives helps to guarantee that one's efforts are focused in the right direction and that one can see clear progress toward one's intended results.

Develop a plan of action

Creating a detailed plan of action may assist individuals and teams in remaining focused on the objectives they have set for themselves. This plan should contain timetables and deadlines for each phase, as well as an overview of the actions that need to be followed to attain the targeted goals.

Individuals and teams are able to maintain their concentration and motivation, as well as prevent the waste of time and resources on activities that do not contribute to the achievement of the intended results, when they have a detailed plan of action to follow.

Prioritize activities

While working towards long-term objectives, it is essential to establish a hierarchy of activities, so that one's efforts may be concentrated on the most vital of the many necessary endeavors. This may be of assistance to both individuals and teams in maintaining their concentration and avoiding being mired down in activities that do not contribute to the accomplishment of the goals that have been set.

Minimize distractions

Reducing distractions to a minimum may assist people and teams in remaining focused on the objectives at hand. This may include restricting the use of social media or email while on the job, or it may involve designing a workplace that is only for work and is free from any potential distractions.

Review progress regularly

Reviewing the progress that has been made towards objectives on a regular basis may assist individuals and teams in remaining on track and making required modifications. This may assist to ensure that efforts are focused towards reaching the targeted results, and it can also help to discover areas that might benefit from development or change.

Assessing the Impact of Cutting the String

Cutting the string or making a difficult choice to remove hurdles may have a big influence on many facets of one's life, including personal relationships, one's professional life, one's financial situation, and one's overall health and well-being. As a result, it is essential to evaluate the impacts of cutting the string and establish whether or not it produced the outcomes that were anticipated. The purpose of this topic is to offer direction on how to evaluate the effects of cutting the string and how to make any required modifications going forward.

Define the goals

It is vital to clarify your goals and objectives before you cut the string, so that you know where you are going. By doing so, you will be able to establish whether or not cutting the string has assisted you in reaching your objectives. Put yourself in your own shoes and ask questions such, "What was the primary issue or roadblock that I was attempting to overcome by cutting the string?" Why did I decide to cut the string? What did I want to accomplish? Does severing the string assist me in achieving these objectives? In the event that this is not the case, what modifications do I need to make?

Identify the metrics

A metric is a particular measurement, and you will use it to evaluate the effect of cutting the string using specified metrics. The specifics of the choice and the objectives you want to accomplish will each have an impact on the measurements. For instance, if you have made the decision to stop a relationship because it is unhealthy for you, some of the metrics you may want to consider are your general happiness, your stress levels, and your self-esteem. If you have made the decision to leave your job and establish a company instead, some of the measures you may choose to focus on include things like revenue, new customer acquisition, and staff happiness.

Collect data

The next stage is to gather data once you have established your objectives and determined the metrics to use. This might entail self-reflection, questionnaires, interviews with stakeholders, and other means of information collection. For instance, if you have severed relations with a toxic buddy, you can think about how you feel now that you are no longer in touch with them. You might also ask other people you know, such as family members or friends, what they think about the shift in your behavior.

Analyze the data

After you have finished collecting the data, the next step is to do an analysis so that you can assess the effects of cutting the string. Examine the information to search for any recurring themes, tendencies, or connections. To establish whether or not you have reached your original goals and objectives, compare the facts to them.

Make adjustments

It's possible that you'll need to modify your strategy in light of the results of your examination of the data. It's possible that this will require you to adjust your objectives, make adjustments to the measurements you're using, or make other adjustments to the way you make decisions. For instance, if you have not been successful in achieving your objectives, you may need to reconsider your choice to cut the string and consider the possibility that there were other aspects of your situation that were responsible for your failure.

Reevaluate periodically

In order to verify that you are on the right path to accomplish what you have set out to do, it is essential to conduct periodic reviews of the effects of cutting the string. Specify a date for when you will reconsider your choice and make any required revisions.

Subsequently, one of the most significant steps in the process of making a choice is to do an analysis of the effects of cutting the string. It enables you to evaluate whether or not you have accomplished your objectives and to make any required modifications. You may guarantee that you are moving ahead in a manner that is congruent with your core beliefs and objectives by setting your goals, selecting measurements, collecting data, analyzing the data, making modifications, and occasionally reevaluating your choice.

Chapter 5

The Benefits of Straightening the String

When we talk about "straightening the string," we are referring to the process of recognizing and eliminating the things in our life that are acting as roadblocks to our progress toward reaching our objectives. These barriers may take various forms, including harmful habits, negative thinking patterns, and toxic relationships, and can inhibit our growth in both our personal and professional life. On the other hand, if we take the time to straighten up our strings, we can get rid of these obstacles, which will allow us to become more effective, productive, and successful.

In this chapter, we will study the various advantages of straightening the string. There are a multitude of benefits that can be attained by taking the time to recognize and get rid of the string that is holding us back, including higher efficiency and production, as well as improved communication and attention. By doing so, we may save time, money, and energy, and eventually attain our objectives more easily

But before we get into the advantages of straightening the string, it's crucial to grasp what this term truly implies. In order for us to correct the crookedness in the string, we will need to take a step back and examine our life from a new angle. It demands us to be truthful with ourselves about our flaws and to recognize the challenges that impede us from making progress. It also demands us to have the fortitude to make difficult choices and severe ties with people, habits, or circumstances that are no longer in our best interests.

The kinks in the string may be worked out, allowing us to regain control of our life and get closer to the success and satisfaction we so desperately want. We have the ability to make more deliberate decisions and give higher priority to the things that are most important. Yet to do so, we must first comprehend the advantages of this practice and be prepared to put in the effort to make it a reality.

Thus, let's investigate the many advantages of straightening the string and discover how we may use this technique into our daily lives to realize our ambitions and lead the fullest possible lives.

Increased Efficiency

Straightening the String Can Lead to Increased Efficiency

The metaphor of "straightening the string" describes the process of determining and eliminating the impediments that stand between us and the accomplishment of our objectives. This may manifest itself in a variety of ways, such as harmful behaviors, negative thought patterns, and toxic relationships. The kinks in the string may be worked out, allowing us to become more effective and productive in our personal and professional life respectively. In this part of the chapter, we will discuss how putting a kink in a string may lead to better efficiency, as well as how you might apply this strategy to your own life in a meaningful way.

Identification of Obstacles

The first thing we need to do in order to get the string back in its proper position is to pinpoint the challenges that stand in the way of reaching our objectives. This might entail everything from putting things off and not being able to concentrate to poisonous relationships and bad self-talk. We may become more effective in our day-to-day lives if we take the time to recognize these challenges, devise solutions for overcoming them, and implement those techniques.

Task Prioritization

Another way that straightening the string might contribute to better productivity is by assisting us in determining the order in which we should complete the chores. When we have a crystal clear grasp of our objectives and the challenges that stand in our way, we are able to determine which activities are the most essential and direct our attention, time, and effort toward accomplishing those activities. Because of this, we won't have to squander time on activities that aren't as important to us, and we'll be able to work more effectively toward our objectives.

Time Management

The act of straightening the string may also assist us in becoming better at managing our time in a productive manner. It is possible for us to design methods that will allow us to make better use of our time if we first identify the barriers that impede us from doing so efficiently and then work to remove those obstacles. This might involve anything from avoiding distractions and delegating chores to taking pauses and engaging in self-care practices.

Communication Improvements

Straightening the string also improves communication, which is another one of its many benefits. It is possible for us to become more successful in our contacts with other people if we first recognize the challenges we have in speaking clearly and then work to overcome those challenges. This might entail everything from enhancing our listening abilities and expressing ourselves effectively to avoiding confrontation and finding solutions to problems in a more timely manner.

Increased Focus

Last but not least, reorienting the string might assist us in developing a sharper focus on our objectives. We may become more effective in reaching our objectives if we get rid of the barriers that cause us to get distracted and stop us from concentrating on the things that really important. This may include a wide range of activities, including but not limited to the establishment of clear priorities and routines, the practice of mindfulness, and the cultivation of a positive mentality.

Subsequently, straightening the string is an effective exercise that may lead to better efficiency in many facets of our life, including the workplace and personal relationships. It is possible for us to become more productive, focused, and successful if we first recognize the barriers that impede us from accomplishing our objectives, and then take the necessary steps to remove those hurdles. You will be able to start straightening up your string and realizing your maximum potential if you put into practice the ideas that are covered in this section.

Examples of Tasks that Become Easier

As we eliminate the kinks in the string and remove the barriers that stand in the way of us accomplishing our objectives, we are able to live lives that are both more productive and less time consuming. This can result in a wide range of advantages, including the simplification of certain responsibilities and activities. In this part of the chapter, we will look at a few instances of jobs that are simplified when performed using a string that has been straightened.

Time Management

Managing our time wisely is vital to attaining our objectives and being more efficient in our everyday life. We will be able to recognize and eliminate the impediments that impede us from efficiently managing our time if we have a string that has been straightened. This might involve everything from avoiding procrastination and establishing crystal-clear objectives to delegating duties and engaging in self-care. When we are able to successfully manage our time, not only are we able to complete activities in a more effective manner, but we are also able to make the most of the time that is available to us.

Decision-Making

Making decisions may be tough, particularly when we are presented with options that are difficult or complicated. We are able to eliminate the obstructions that prohibit us from making good selections with the help of a string that has been straightened. This may include a wide range of goals, including as lowering levels of stress and anxiety, enhancing our capacity for critical thinking, and cultivating a more optimistic outlook. When we are better equipped to make judgments in a timely manner, we are able to avoid squandering time and effort on paralysis by analysis and instead go on with self-assurance.

Communication

Building lasting connections and accomplishing our objectives both need effective communication. We are able to eliminate the hurdles that impede us from communicating successfully by using a string that has been straightened. This might entail everything from enhancing our listening abilities and expressing ourselves effectively to avoiding confrontation and finding solutions to problems in a more timely manner. When we are able to communicate clearly, not only are we better able to prevent misunderstandings with other people, but we may also strengthen the ties we have with them.

Productivity

When it comes to reaching our objectives and making headway in both our personal and professional lives, productivity is very necessary. We are now able to eliminate the roadblocks that are preventing us from being productive by using a string that has been straightened. This may include anything from avoiding distractions and developing routines to delegating duties and engaging in self-care. When we are able to be more productive, we are able to do more tasks in a shorter amount of time and make the most of the resources that are available to us.

Self-Improvement

The general health and happiness of a person are directly correlated to their level of personal development and commitment to self-improvement. We are able to get rid of the roadblocks that are preventing us from accomplishing our own objectives when we straighten up the string. This may include a wide range of practices, such as cultivating good habits, working on increasing our self-esteem, practicing mindfulness, and placing an emphasis on self-care. We have the potential to become more robust, confident, and satisfied when we are free to concentrate on our own personal development.

Advancement in Career

To advance in our jobs and achieve success in our professional lives, we need to put in a lot of effort, devote ourselves fully, and carefully plan our next steps. If we can get the string straightened up, we can get rid of the impediments that are preventing us from accomplishing our professional objectives. This might entail everything from enhancing our time management and communication skills to building a solid professional network and continuing our education. We have the potential to become more competitive, self-assured, and successful in our professional life when we are able to concentrate on the progression of our careers.

Subsequently, straightening the string may result in a range of advantages, one of which is the facilitation of the completion of certain activities. We will be able to do more in a shorter amount of time and make the most of the resources that we have at our disposal if we eliminate the barriers that stop us from reaching our objectives and become more efficient. You will be able to start straightening up your string and making your chores much simpler to complete if you put the ideas outlined in this part to use.

Importance of Understanding the Benefits

It is essential to have a complete comprehension of the perks that are associated with the process of straightening the string before making any attempts to do so. This comprehension not only helps to motivate oneself to put in the necessary amount of work and resources for the process, but it also contributes to the prioritization of the activities that need to be carried out.

Increasing productivity is one of the most important advantages that may be gained by straightening the string. After the string is straightened, the obstructions that were making it difficult to make progress are eliminated, which makes it simpler to complete the chores that need to be done. This may be seen in a wide variety of facets of life, including personal relationships, the operations of a company, and personal objective

When it comes to personal relationships, getting the string back in its proper place may lead to increased communication and understanding between partners. It may be challenging to keep a good relationship going when there are roadblocks in the shape of unsolved problems or misunderstandings. Couples may, however, build a better and more satisfying relationship by recognizing and resolving these challenges.

When it comes to the operations of a company, pulling the string in the right direction may lead to increased production and profitability. For instance, a company can discover that there are inefficiencies in its manufacturing process or supply chain that are preventing them from reaching their full potential. They may raise their production while also lowering their expenses, which will ultimately lead to an increase in their profitability, if they solve these challenges and streamline their processes.

When it comes to one's own objectives, pulling the string in the right direction may assist an individual realize their ambitions. For instance, a person who has been having trouble saving money may see impediments such as excessive spending or a lack of a budget as a problem. They may reach their objective of financial stability by overcoming these challenges and devising a strategy for saving money.

Nonetheless, it is essential to keep in mind that the process of straightening the string is not a one-time event. Maintaining the advantages that have been attained requires continual work and attention. For instance, a company that has successfully simplified its operations would need to continue to evaluate their procedures and make modifications as necessary to ensure that they are successful in the long run.

In addition, it is essential to have a clear understanding of the fact that the advantages of straightening the string may not always be immediately apparent. It is possible that it may take some time before we see the fruits of our labor in terms of eliminating hurdles and simplifying procedures. The rewards, however, may be substantial and long-lasting if one is patient and persistent in their pursuit of them.

Understanding the advantages of straightening the string is, without a doubt, an essential first step in the process, as the whole picture makes it abundantly evident. Individuals and organizations may increase their productivity and level of success in their undertakings by first recognizing the challenges that are preventing forward movement and then actively working to overcome those challenges.

Improved Communication

Straightened String can Improve Communication

Communication is crucial in any form of company to make sure that everyone is working towards the same goals and objectives. As the kinks in the string are worked out, communication is improved, which in turn leads to improved decision-making, more cooperation, and increased productivity. Straightening the string may enhance communication in a variety of different ways, all of which will be covered in this portion of the section.

Clearer Roles and Duties

When there is a tangle in the string, it might be difficult to determine who is accountable for what. Because of this, there is a possibility of confusion, misunderstanding, and errors. In order to get the string back in order, you will need to define clear roles and duties for everyone involved. This will make it much simpler for everyone to understand what it is that they are responsible for. When everyone is aware of their responsibilities, they are able to interact with one another more efficiently.

Improved Clarity

When there is a tangle in the string, it might be difficult to grasp what a person is attempting to communicate. Because of this, there is a possibility of misunderstandings and errors. The communication gets more evident as the string is straightened. Individuals can communicate themselves more clearly, and others can grasp what they are saying more readily. This not only enhances the quality of communication, but it also lessens the possibility that misunderstandings and errors will occur.

Improved Cooperation

When there are too many knots in the string, it might be challenging for individuals to collaborate efficiently. It is possible that they do not comprehend one other's duties or what it is that they are attempting to accomplish. This may lead to disagreements, delays, and errors. Improving communication will lead to enhanced teamwork, which will be necessary to straighten out the kinks in the string. Individuals are able to collaborate more successfully when they have a mutual understanding of their respective responsibilities and of the goals they are working toward. This results in improved decision-making as well as a more efficient workflow.

Increased Trust

People may lose faith in one another when the string gets twisted. Someone can believe that another person is accountable for something, only to discover afterwards that they were mistaken. This might result in a lack of trust and collaboration among the parties involved. People may trust one another more when the string is straightened. They are able to depend on one another to get things done because they have a clear understanding of who is accountable for what. This contributes to a more upbeat and productive atmosphere at work.

Better Feedback

When there is a tangle in the string, it might be difficult to convey feedback in an effective manner. Individuals could not comprehend what it is that they are meant to be doing, or they might not be aware of how to make improvements. Improving communication, which ultimately results in more useful feedback, is necessary to straighten up the string. Individuals are able to comprehend what it is that they should be doing, and they are able to get feedback that is not just understandable but also practical. This results in a feedback loop that is more effective, which in turn leads to greater performance.

Better Relationships

It might be challenging to establish new connections when there is a tangle in the string. It's possible that people don't trust one other, and it's also possible that they don't comprehend each other's positions or goals. Improving communication can help you have stronger connections, which is an important step towards straightening up the string. People are able to better understand one another, and they are able to develop deeper relationships based on trust and collaboration with one another. This contributes to a more upbeat and productive atmosphere at work.

To summarize, pulling the string in the right direction may have a big effect on the communication that occurs inside a company. As the kinks in the string are worked out, communication is improved, which in turn leads to improved decision-making, more cooperation, and increased productivity. Organizations may take action to enhance communication and more successfully accomplish their objectives if they have a solid knowledge of the advantages that will result from straightening the string.

Occurrence of Miscommunication in Tangled String

When the string gets twisted, it might be difficult to create effective communication, which is a fundamental component of any business; yet, effective communication is necessary. As the string becomes knotted, information is lost, and there is a greater chance that messages will be misconstrued or misread, which can lead to a breakdown in communication. Miscommunication may result in a wide variety of issues, ranging from little misunderstandings to significant disagreements, delays, and errors.

Confusion is one of the primary contributors to misunderstandings in communication when there is a tangled string. If numerous persons are accountable for a work or project, but it is unclear who is responsible for what, it may result in confusion, duplication of effort, or duties that are not completed. Because of this miscommunication, employees may end themselves working on things that are not their responsibility, which results in delays and irritation for everyone involved.

Incomplete or erroneous information is another factor that might contribute to misunderstanding. As the string becomes knotted, there is a greater chance that information will be lost or misconstrued as it is sent via a variety of persons and channels. This may lead to misconceptions, assumptions, or false assumptions, which might create difficulties down the road.

When individuals perceive the same information in different ways, misunderstanding may also happen. This might occur when the communication is ambiguous or obscure, or when individuals have different viewpoints, priorities, or values. It may be difficult to harmonize these multiple meanings when the string gets twisted, which may lead to disputes or conflicts.

It is necessary to untangle the string in order to better communication since there is a possibility that misunderstandings may occur if the string is twisted. Establishing clear routes of communication, clearly delineating roles and duties, and making certain that information is conveyed properly and in its whole are all necessary steps in the process of straightening the string.

When the kinks in the string are worked out, everyone is clear on who is in charge of what, and information can be exchanged in a timely and effective manner. This may assist to avoid misunderstanding and duplication of effort, as well as ensuring that everyone is working toward the same objective. In addition, good communication may assist to develop trust and prevent disputes by ensuring that everyone is aware of what is expected of them and that they can depend on one another to fulfill their responsibilities.

Putting the knot in the string in a straighter position may help promote communication by fostering an atmosphere of openness and transparency. When everyone is aware of what is taking place and has easy access to information, it may be beneficial to the development of a feeling of trust and collaboration. When individuals feel heard and respected, they are more inclined to offer their ideas and comments, which in turn may lead to improved cooperation, problem-solving, and creativity.

Another advantage of straightening the string is that it may assist in improving communication with external stakeholders, such as customers or suppliers. This is a potential benefit of straightening the string. It is possible to project an image to the outside world that is uniform and professional when all members of the company are on the same page and efficiently communicate with one another. This may assist to develop deeper connections with consumers and suppliers, which can lead to better results for everyone involved.

Miscommunication is a prevalent difficulty when the string is tangled, and it may lead to a wide variety of difficulties, from slight misunderstandings to big disputes and blunders. Subsequently, when the string is twisted, the most common problem is miscommunication. It is crucial to straighten the string in order to enhance communication since doing so may help create clear roles and responsibilities, ensuring that information is shared in an accurate and full manner, and promote trust and transparency. It is possible for businesses to establish a culture of good communication, which in turn leads to improved results for everyone involved if the string is only straightened up.

Examples of how a straightened string can help individuals be more productive

Getting one's string straightened up may assist a person in being more productive in a variety of different ways. Individuals may save time, energy, and money by eliminating barriers and simplifying procedures, which enables them to concentrate on what is most important to them. In this section, we will examine several instances of how people might benefit from having a straighter string in order to become more productive.

Clear Priorities and Goals

Individuals might have more focused objectives and goals when their string is straight. Individuals can simply recognize what has to be done and in what sequence when there are no tangles or obstructions in the way. Because of this clarity, people may be able to become more productive by cutting down on confusion and lowering the amount of time and effort that is spent.

Effective Time Management

The ability to manage one's time in a more effective manner is another benefit that comes from having one's string straightened. Individuals may more efficiently arrange their time and allocate resources when they have defined objectives and goals. This may result in improved time management and higher levels of productivity, which in turn enables people to do more in a shorter amount of time.

Better Communication

Productivity depends on clear and effective communication. When people straighten a string, it may help them communicate more effectively by reducing the number of misconceptions that occur and enhancing the level of clarity that is achieved. Communication is facilitated and productivity is increased when all parties involved have a clear understanding of what must be completed, by whom, and by when.

Improved Decision Making

The process of decision-making may also be helped by giving the string a good straightening. When there are no obstructions or tangles, people are better able to examine their alternatives, think about the possible repercussions, and make judgments based on that information. This may result in improved results as well as an increase in production.

Enhanced Collaboration

For successful results, collaboration is often required. The ability to straighten a string may improve teamwork by reducing the number of misconceptions and increasing the amount of clear communication. Collaboration is more successful and productivity rises when all parties involved have a clear understanding of their positions and the obligations that come with them, and when communication is unimpeded.

Streamlined Processes

A procedure that has been straightened out may also assist simplify other processes, which can make those processes more effective and productive. This can be accomplished with the use of a straightened string. Individuals may save time and effort, enabling them to concentrate on the activities that are most important to them, if they first recognize and then get rid of any needless phases in a process. This has the potential to lead to higher levels of productivity and greater results.

Improved Focus

Subsequently, a string that has been straightened may assist folks in keeping their attention. People are better able to focus on the work at hand without getting sidetracked by other concerns when there are no tangles or barriers in the way. This may lead to improvements in attention as well as increases in productivity and overall quality of results.

To summarize, a string that has been straightened may assist folks in being more productive in a variety of ways. Individuals may save time, energy, and money by eliminating barriers and simplifying procedures, which enables them to concentrate on what is most important to them. Individuals may become more productive if they have clear objectives and goals, effective time management, greater communication, enhanced cooperation, simplified procedures, and improved concentration. These are just some of the ways in which a straightened string can benefit people.

Enhanced Focus

Focus is very necessary if one want to accomplish their objectives and raise their level of productivity. A string that has been straightened out may be an effective tool for improving concentration and attaining one's goals. In the following paragraphs, we will discuss the idea of attention, its significance, and how adjusting the tension in the string may assist you in achieving higher levels of focus as well as productivity.

Let's determine focus first. The capacity to concentrate on a single job or goal while filtering out distractions and other competing objectives is what we mean when we talk about having focus. It is much too simple to allow oneself to get sidetracked and lose concentration in the modern world with its hectic pace. Social media, email, phone calls, and other distractions may make it difficult to complete our tasks and reach our objectives.

It is impossible to exaggerate the value of concentration. When we are able to concentrate, our levels of productivity, efficiency, and effectiveness all increase. We can do more in a shorter amount of time and with less work, which may ultimately lead to more success and contentment.

Hence, how exactly does straightening the string aid improve one's ability to focus? One of the most significant advantages of straightening the string is that it enables us to prioritize our responsibilities and get rid of distractions that aren't required. When there is a knot in the string, it might be difficult to differentiate between activities that are urgent and those that are significant. We may find ourselves bouncing from one activity to another, without ever actually making progress on anything.

Nevertheless, when we straighten out the string, we can more quickly recognize the activities that are the most essential to us and direct our attention and resources toward completing those chores. We may also reduce unneeded distractions and interruptions, such as phone calls, email alerts, and messages from social networking platforms, which can pull our attention away from the task at hand and make it harder for us to concentrate.

The following are some particular instances in which a string that has been straightened might aid boost one's ability to focus:

Prioritization

When everything is in its proper place, it will be much simpler for us to isolate and prioritize the activities that are of the utmost importance to us. This is known as the string theory. We have the ability to clearly plan out what needs to be done and when it needs to be done, which may assist us in staying on track and maintaining our concentration.

Time management

The ability to manage our time more efficiently may also be facilitated by a string that has been straightened. We may do more in less time and with less work if we get rid of the unneeded distractions and concentrate on the most essential things at hand.

Stress reduction

When we are able to maintain our attention and get things done, we experience less stress and a greater sense of mastery. By eliminating distractions and making it easier for us to focus on the job at hand, a string that has been straightened may assist us in reaching this level of peaceful concentration.

Increased creativity

Lastly, a string that has been straightened may also serve to promote creative thinking. Our thoughts are more open and sensitive to fresh ideas and inspiration when we are focused and free from distractions. As our string is straightened, it's possible that we'll discover that we're able to produce more original and imaginative answers to the issues we're facing.

In summation, attention is vital for obtaining success and contentment in our life. By reorienting the string, we will be able to improve our ability to concentrate and productivity by assigning higher priority to our work, better managing our time, experiencing less stress, and having more creative ideas. You may want to attempt straightening your string so that you can experience the advantages for yourself if you're interested in achieving higher levels of success and contentment in your life.

A Tangled String can be Distracting

When we have a lot of different activities and duties to take care of, it may be challenging to maintain our concentration and keep on track with everything. A tangled string of chores, deadlines, and priorities may be distracting and daunting. The following is a list of the many ways that a twisted string might be distracting:

Mental clutter

When there are too many things competing for our attention, it may be challenging to concentrate on any one particular job. It might be difficult to focus on any one item when there is a tangled string of activities and obligations.

Stress

A knotted string is another potential cause of stress in the workplace. It is fairly uncommon for us to feel stressed and overburdened when we have an excessive amount of work to do but insufficient time to complete it.

Procrastination

When we have a lot of things to accomplish, we often feel immobilized and have no idea where to begin. This might lead to procrastination, which further complicates an already complicated situation.

Multitasking

When we have a lot on our plate, we could get the impression that we have to multitask in order to get everything done. But, it is possible that we will not give our whole attention to any one of the tasks if we are multitasking, which may be a distraction in and of itself.

Overall, a tangled string of activities and obligations may be a huge source of distraction and stress, making it difficult to remain focused and effective. This is because of the increased likelihood of forgetting anything important.

On the other side, a string that has been straightened may increase attention and productivity since it reveals a distinct way to go ahead. When we have a clear grasp of our objectives and the measures we need to take to attain our goals, it becomes simpler to remain focused and productive.

The following are some of the ways in which a string that has been straightened might improve focus:

Clarity

Clarity is provided by a string that has been straightened, assisting us in determining our priorities and the measures we need to take in order to reach our objectives. Because of this, it may become less difficult to concentrate on what is important and steer clear of distractions.

Time management

The ability to manage our time more efficiently may also be facilitated by a string that has been straightened. When we have a crystal clear grasp of our priorities, we are better able to organize our time effectively, which allows us to ensure that we are devoting our time to the activities that are most important to us.

Motivation

A straightened string may be motivational because it gives a clear route ahead and a feeling of success as we finish each job. This is because a straightened string provides a clear way forward. Even when confronted with challenging or monotonous jobs, this may assist us in maintaining our attention and productivity.

Stress reduction

When we have a string that has been straightened, we are able to approach our duties and obligations with a higher level of self-assurance and a lower level of tension. When we are aware of what has to be done and how it should be done, we are less likely to have sensations of being overwhelmed or anxious.

Overall, a straightened string may improve concentration and productivity by offering clarity, enhancing time management, boosting motivation, and lowering stress. This is because a straightened string is more visually appealing. We may accomplish our objectives more quickly and with fewer interruptions by organizing our string of chores and obligations.

Examples of how communication can be improved with a straightened string

Communication is an essential part of both one's personal and professional lives, and the quality of communication may be significantly improved by simply pulling the string in the other direction. Communication may become difficult when a string gets twisted, which can lead to misconceptions, which can lead to complications and slow down work. On the other side, a string that has been straightened may increase communication and productivity, which in turn makes it simpler to accomplish objectives and function in an effective manner.

The following are some instances in which a string that has been straightened might enhance communication:

Improved Directions

When there is a tangle in the string, it might be difficult to grasp what is being requested of you or to offer precise directions. Because of this, there is a possibility of misunderstandings and errors. Instructions may be communicated more clearly, and the person receiving them will have an easier time comprehending them if the string is straightened. This may result in a more effective working process and prevent errors that might impede development.

Better Collaboration

Collaboration is crucial in most businesses, but it may be tough to work together efficiently when there is a twisted string. For instance, if two individuals are working on a project together and the string becomes knotted, they could discover that they are continually getting in each other's way or that they are unable to communicate effectively with one another. When a string is straightened, it makes it simpler to collaborate, which in turn makes it possible for members of a team to work together more successfully and efficiently.

More Effective Meetings

A twisted string may render a meeting ineffective and irritating, despite the fact that meetings are an essential component of any organization. Important ideas may be overlooked or misconstrued because participants may get preoccupied. In order to make meetings more productive and ensure that everyone is on the same page, the string has to be straightened. Decisions may be taken more rapidly and discussions can be more transparent, which can lead to time savings and an increase in productivity.

Improved Relationships

Building successful connections, whether they be personal or professional, requires effective communication.

It is sometimes difficult to communicate effectively when a string gets knotted, which may result in misunderstandings and put a strain on relationships. The ability to communicate clearly and effectively is one of the most important factors in the success of any relationship. Individuals are able to have a deeper understanding of one another, which may result in improved relationships and increased productivity while working together.

Increased Efficiency

The ability to communicate effectively is essential to maximizing productivity, and a reorganized string may make a significant contribution to this goal. When communication is clear and effective, activities may be accomplished more quickly and precisely, which can save time and boost productivity. For instance, if an employee is given a job and is able to comprehend it completely, they will be able to do it in a more efficient manner since they will not need to stop and ask for clarification on the instructions.

Subsequently, a string that has been straightened may significantly increase both communication and productivity in one's personal life as well as one's work life. A few instances of how a straightened string may improve communication include providing directions that are easier to understand, improving cooperation, holding meetings that are more productive, improving relationships, and increasing efficiency. Individuals and organizations may more quickly and successfully accomplish their objectives if they place a greater emphasis on enhancing their communication and working to straighten out the knots in the string.

Increased Productivity

Productivity is often one of the most crucial variables when it comes to reaching achievement. The capacity to complete responsibilities and realize objectives in a timely and effective way is what we mean when we talk about productivity. As our string is straightened, we will be able to dramatically improve the amount of work that we get done. In this chapter, we will talk about how adjusting the tension on the string may result in higher production.

To begin, it is essential to have a good understanding of the effect that a twisted string may have on the amount of work that can be accomplished. A string that is twisted up might lead to confusion, which makes it more difficult to locate the correct route. As a result of this uncertainty, people may find themselves wasting time and effort as they try to untangle the string and figure out the most effective next step. On the other side, a string that has been straightened may bring clarity and direction, making it simpler for folks to concentrate on the activities at hand and work effectively toward achieving their objectives.

The workplace is one instance where having a crooked string straightened up may lead to increased productivity. Productivity will be higher at a firm that has a clear and well-defined mission statement and strategic objectives than at a company that lacks focus or direction. When employees have a clear understanding of the overarching goals of the organization, they will be better able to prioritize their work and make efficient use of the time they have available. Because of this clarity, workers will have a better chance of working together on projects, as they will have a common grasp of the goals toward which they are striving.

Personal life is another illustration of how a straightened string might boost one's overall productivity. For instance, a person who is attempting to do a number of chores within the span of a single day is at risk of rapidly being overwhelmed if their priorities have not been properly established. It is easy to squander time and effort on less essential things if one does not have a crystal clear idea of what must be completed first. They will be able to obtain a better knowledge of their priorities and direct their efforts more effectively toward the most critical tasks at hand if they first straighten their string.

Productivity also relies heavily on one's ability to effectively manage their time. A knotted string might make it difficult to efficiently manage time, which can result in missed deadlines and opportunities that were missed out on. Individuals are better able to organize their day, assign higher priority to their duties, and make more effective use of their time when they have a string that has been straightened. This can help them to stay on track and meet their deadlines, ultimately leading to greater productivity.

In addition, a string that has been straightened may assist persons in determining and avoiding activities that waste their time. We may waste time on activities that are not necessary or that do not advance our objectives when our string gets twisted. We are able to concentrate on the activities that are really vital to us and get rid of the distractions that aren't required if we only straighten up our string. This may assist us in working more effectively and making the most of the time we have available.

Subsequently, a string that has been straightened up might result in enhanced motivation and engagement. We are more likely to be motivated to succeed when we have a clear grasp of what we are working towards and how to reach our objectives. This drive may lead to a higher level of involvement in our job, as well as a greater feeling of pleasure as we progress toward achieving our objectives. In the end, this feeling of accomplishment may further improve our productivity and feed our ambition to succeed.

A Tangled String can lead to Wasted Time and Resources

A tangled string, in the context of the "Straighten Your Strings" paradigm, refers to any barrier or inefficiency that prevents a person or organization from reaching their objectives. In the event that these challenges are not handled, they have the potential to result in lost time and resources, both of which may have a detrimental effect on production and achievement.

A tangled string may result in lost time and resources in a number of fundamental ways, one of the most significant of which is by producing labor that is not essential. For instance, if a person is working on a project but is continually interrupted by incoming emails or phone calls, it is possible that they will need to repeatedly redirect their attention, which will cause the activity to take much longer to finish. This may lead to lost time and energy that might have been spent on more productive pursuits.

Another way that a tangled string might result in lost time and resources is by delaying the completion of the task at hand. It is possible for there to be unneeded delays in the timetable of the project if, for instance, a person is waiting on a response or permission from a colleague, but that colleague is not communicating effectively or is ignoring the problem. These delays may be expensive, since they may need more resources or lead the project to miss a vital date.

In addition, a knotted string may lead to wasted resources by producing misunderstanding or miscommunication, which in turn can lead to further lost resources. Misunderstandings, work that is duplicated, or work that is not in alignment with the general aims of the project may all result from a person or team not communicating properly. This may result in lost time and resources that might have been utilized more efficiently if everyone was on the same page.

A tangled string may have a substantial influence on overall productivity and success by resulting in lost time and resources. This can be caused by the inability to untangle the string. In order to simplify procedures and make progress toward objectives in a more timely manner, it is critical to recognize and eliminate the barriers that stand in the way. Individuals and organizations may decrease the amount of time and resources that are spent by straightening up the string and resolving these inefficiencies, and they can concentrate their attention on accomplishing their objectives as a result.

Examples of how a straightened string can help individuals be more productive

People may become more productive in a number of ways with the aid of a string that has been straightened. Here are several examples:

- A Straight String Makes It Easier to See What Needs to be done and Prioritize Tasks When the string is straight, it is simpler to see what needs to be done and prioritize chores. Individuals are better able to concentrate on the most essential activities and avoid spending time on things that aren't as vital when they have well defined priorities.

- Effective Time Management A straight string provides people with the ability to more successfully plan how they will use their time. Users are able to see the tasks that need to be accomplished as well as the amount of time that is available for each work. They are able to avoid getting off course as a result of this, which is helpful.

- A Straighter String Allows for Better Decision Making: When people have a string that has been straightened, they are able to make better judgments on what jobs to take on and which ones to delegate or delete. They are also able to make more informed choices on the distribution of their time and resources.

- Reduced Stress: Having a string that is knotted may be unpleasant and overpowering, which can lead to postponing or avoiding the task at hand. Individuals are able to feel more in control of their jobs and obligations when the string is straight, which leads to a reduction in tension and anxiety for such persons.

- A straightened string may assist people in remaining focused on their jobs and avoiding distractions, resulting in improved concentration. They are able to work more productively since they are not distracted by other duties or interruptions.

- Increased Productivity: Another benefit of straightening a string is an increase in productivity while working with others. With clear objectives and efficient time management, people may work more successfully with others and accomplish greater outcomes as a team.

- Improved Motivation: A straightened string may provide a distinct feeling of progress and success, which can lead to a rise in one's level of motivation. Individuals are able to monitor their progress when activities are performed, which motivates them to keep working toward their objectives.

Overall, a straightened string may help people be more productive by offering clarity, increasing efficiency, and focusing their attention on the task at hand. By reducing impediments and becoming more efficient, people may save time, money, and energy, and eventually attain their objectives more easily.

Improved Relationships

Straightening the string may have a significant influence not only on increased efficiency, productivity, and concentration, but also on the quality of one's personal and professional connections. When people are able to successfully express their aims and priorities to others, it may lead to improved relationships with those people. This chapter will explain the ways in which straightening the string may strengthen relationships, including how it can improve communication, promote trust and respect, and create cooperation and collaboration.

The ability to communicate more effectively is one of the key ways in which improving relationships may be accomplished by "straightening the string." When people have a crystal clear grasp of their own objectives and priorities, they are better able to convey this information to others, which ultimately leads to improved communication. For instance, when members of a team have a crystal clear understanding of their individual responsibilities and goals, they are better able to communicate with one another about how their work connects to that of the rest of the team and how they can best support one another in order to achieve the team's overall objectives. Also, when people are able to convey their own needs and priorities, they are better able to listen and comprehend the needs and priorities of others, which may lead to more successful cooperation and problem-solving.

One further method that straightening the string may strengthen relationships is by increasing levels of trust and respect between the parties involved. When people are able to properly articulate their own objectives and priorities, and are able to match these with the goals and priorities of others, it may lead to enhanced trust and respect amongst team members. This is because when people feel that their own needs and objectives are being acknowledged and respected, they are more inclined to return this respect and trust towards others. In addition, when members of a team are able to successfully collaborate toward the accomplishment of shared objectives, it often results in an increased feeling of camaraderie as well as mutual respect.

The process of straightening the string may also encourage cooperation and teamwork, both of which can have a beneficial effect on interpersonal connections. When members of a team are able to effectively communicate about their work and are aware of their respective roles and responsibilities, they are better equipped to work together to accomplish the team's collective objectives. In addition, when people have a good grasp of their own strengths and shortcomings, they are better able to collaborate with others who have talents and qualities that complement their own. This may lead to more cooperation and teamwork since people are able to concentrate on their own areas of competence while depending on the contributions of others in areas where they may not be as strong.

In addition, re-straightening the string may result in a heightened awareness of one's own accountability and responsibility, which, in turn, can enhance relationships by promoting an environment that is characterized by trust and mutual assistance. When people are clear on their own objectives and priorities, and are responsible for their own work, they are more likely to take ownership of their work and be accountable to others for completing their obligations. This may develop to a culture of mutual support and trust among members of the team, in which individuals are ready to step in and help one other when it is necessary since they are aware that everyone is working toward the same objectives.

In addition to these advantages, putting the knot in the string back in its proper place may also contribute to a higher feeling of contentment and pleasure in one's relationships. When people are able to communicate well, cooperate efficiently, and work towards common objectives, they are more likely to experience a feeling of achievement and pleasure in their job. In addition, people are more likely to experience feelings of fulfillment and satisfaction in their interactions with others when they believe that their specific requirements and priorities are being recognized and respected.

It is essential to keep in mind, however, that straightening the string is not a one-time activity but rather a continuing process that calls for constant attention and effort on the part of the person doing the straightening. It is essential for people to do regular self-evaluations of their objectives and priorities, as well as to successfully convey them to others. In addition to this, it is essential for the members of the team to regularly evaluate the collective objectives and priorities they have set for themselves, and then to work together in an efficient and cooperative way in order to accomplish these objectives.

Conclusion

The book concludes by exploring the problem of workarounds, their costs, and the need of removing them. It analyzes the numerous sorts of workarounds, both technological and behavioral, and the psychology underlying their usage, such as fear of repercussions and aversion to change. The book also illustrates the detrimental effect of workarounds on productivity and morale and the long-term expenses connected with them.

The book advises identifying hurdles, creating clear communication and accountability mechanisms, and eliminating workarounds as a means of accomplishing this goal. It also offers strategies for evaluating the effect of challenges and making difficult choices, such as working together, using a data-driven approach, and striking a balance between risks and rewards. The necessity of cutting the string, determining which strings need to be cut, and the variables that should be considered when deciding whether or not to cut a string are all discussed in depth throughout the book.

In addition, the book offers methods for effectively explaining difficult choices to stakeholders and coping with opposition and reaction. In addition to that, it offers advice on how to deal with negative criticism and how to proceed after the string has been cut, such as evaluating the effects of the decision and maintaining a focus on one's objectives.

There are a lot of different and substantial advantages that come with straightening up the string. The repositioning of the knots on the string may result in higher effectiveness, which in turn can lead to improved communication, enhanced attention, increased productivity, and enhanced relationships. The book gives specific instances of errands that are made simpler by using a straightened string, as well as ways in which people might become more productive by using a straightened string.

In general, the book emphasizes how important it is to do rid of workarounds and cut the string in order to boost production and morale. It includes valuable tactics and procedures for finding and analyzing barriers, making challenging choices, conveying harsh conclusions, and handling opposition and backlash. In addition to this, it highlights the advantages of straightening the string and includes illustrations of how doing so may improve communication, boost attention, and improve relationships. Anybody who wants to increase the efficiency, productivity, and morale in their company should read this book since it is an invaluable resource.